My Catholic Faith!

My Catholic Faith!

Volume One of Three

My Catholic Life! Series

By

John Paul Thomas

My Catholic Life! Inc.
www.myCatholic.Life

ISBN-10: 0692511598
ISBN-13: 978-0692511596

This third revision contains minor formatting differences from the previous versions. The content has not been changed. Page numbering is slightly altered.

The third revision was first printed by Ritman University Press, 104 B Umuahia Road, Ikot Ekpene, Akwa Ibom State, Nigeria.

Imprimatur:
Most Reverend Camillus Raymond Umoh
Catholic Bishop of Ikot Ekpene Diocese
1 December, 2019
First Sunday of Advent, Year A

Nihil Obstat:
Rt. Rev. Msgr. J. F. Iyire
Vicar General
Ikot Ekpene Diocese

Dedication

To our Blessed Mother. Her maternal care for us, her perfect surrender to the will of God and her powerful intercession are gifts beyond measure. May her heart shine through these pages and may her faith be shared with all who read them.

By

John Paul Thomas

"John Paul Thomas" is a pen name this author picked in honor of the Apostles Saints John and Thomas and the great evangelist Saint Paul. This name also evokes the memory of the great Pope Saint John Paul II.

John is the beloved Apostle who sought out a deeply personal and intimate relationship with his Savior. Hopefully the writings in this book point us all to a deeply personal and intimate relationship with our God. May John be a model of this intimacy and love.

Thomas is also a beloved Apostle and close friend of Jesus but is well known for his lack of faith in Jesus' resurrection. Though he ultimately entered into a profound faith crying out "my Lord and my God," he is given to us as a model of our own weakness of faith. Thomas should inspire us to always return to faith when we realize we have doubted.

As a Pharisee, Paul severely persecuted the early Christian Church. However, after going through a powerful conversion, he went on to become the great evangelist to the gentiles, founding many new communities of believers and writing many letters contained in Sacred Scripture. His letters are deeply personal and reveal a shepherd's heart. Paul is a model for all as we seek to embrace our calling to spread the Gospel.

My Catholic Life! Series

An introduction to this three-volume series

The *My Catholic Life! Series* is a three-volume series written as a complete summary of our glorious Catholic faith! The goal of these books is to answer the difficult and deep questions of life in a clear and understandable way. We need to know who we are and what life is all about. We need to know who God is and what He has spoken to us through the ages.

Volume One, *My Catholic Faith!*, is a summary of the Apostles' and Nicene Creeds. This volume looks at everything from the creation of the world to God's eternal plan of salvation. Other topics include: the afterlife, the Trinity, saints, our Blessed Mother, faith, and the Church. It is a summary of the teaching of the *Catechism of the Catholic Church* #1–1065.

Volume Two, *My Catholic Worship!*, is a summary of the life of grace found in prayer and the Sacraments. So often the Sacraments can be seen as dry and empty rituals. But they are, in reality, the greatest treasures we have! They are God's true presence among us! This book is a summary of the *Catechism of the Catholic Church* #1066–1690 and #2558–2865.

Volume Three, *My Catholic Morals!*, is a summary of Catholic moral teaching. It reveals the moral principles of our faith as well as a summary of all our Church's moral teachings. It is a summary of the *Catechism of the Catholic Church* #1691–2557.

Table of Contents

Introduction

There are many beliefs that people have held throughout the ages. But what is common to people of every time and culture is a longing for truth. We want to know! We want to know the purpose of our life, why we are here on earth, where we came from, whether there is a God, who this God is, whether there is an afterlife, and so much more!

These most basic and fundamental questions are hopefully in the forefront of our minds. And if they are not, it's never too late to start! Below is the answer to these questions. It is our Creed. At first, the Creed can seem dry and unimpressive. It can even seem confusing and overly academic. But when properly understood, the Creed holds the answer to the questions we so deeply seek.

The Nicene Creed was written over 1,500 years ago. Since that time, it has been professed, lived and loved by countless Christians and saints of God. It's a summary of our foundational set of beliefs for which, over the centuries, many have even shed their blood. It's deep, profound, clear and transformative when properly understood.

This Creed is professed every Sunday at every Catholic Mass throughout the world. It's said in unison with every other Catholic. But it's also said individually, by each one making the profession. Our individual profession of this faith is what unites us with each other and with our Triune God.

Too often we stand and profess this Creed, and our mind wanders to other things. We think about yesterday or what we will do later in the day. We think about our particular struggles or hurts. Or we may even find ourselves randomly daydreaming as we speak the words of the Creed. I believe the primary reason we can so easily be distracted and enter into "routine mode" as we profess the Creed is because we do not understand it. Sure, we may get the basic parts, but most Catholics do not truly understand the depth and splendor of the Creed. Therefore, most Catholics do not understand the depth and the splendor of their own personal Catholic faith!

If this is you, even to a small degree, then commit yourself to a more in-depth reflection on the faith of the Catholic Church, and continually ask yourself, "Do I believe?"; "Is this also my personal faith?" Be open. Be attentive to God's voice. Seek the truth and let that truth speak to your conscience.

So join along in a reflection on the beautiful answers to the questions of life!

The Creed

I believe in one God, the Father almighty, maker of heaven and earth, of all things visible and invisible.

I believe in one Lord Jesus Christ, the Only Begotten Son of God, born of the Father before all ages. God from God, Light from Light, true God from true God, begotten, not made, consubstantial with the Father; through him all things were made. For us men and for our salvation he came down from heaven, and by the Holy Spirit was incarnate of the Virgin Mary, and became man. For our sake he was crucified under Pontius Pilate, he suffered death and was buried, and rose again on the third day in accordance with the Scriptures. He ascended into heaven and is seated at the right hand of the Father. He will come again in glory to judge the living and the dead and his kingdom will have no end.

I believe in the Holy Spirit, the Lord, the giver of life, who proceeds from the Father and the Son, who with the Father and the Son is adored and glorified, who has spoken through the prophets. I believe in one, holy, catholic and apostolic Church. I confess one Baptism for the forgiveness of sins and I look forward to the resurrection of the dead and the life of the world to come. Amen

1

Coming to Faith

I Believe...

> We begin our profession of faith by saying: "I believe" or "We believe."
> Before expounding the Church's faith, as confessed in the Creed,
> celebrated in the liturgy, and lived in observance of God's commandments
> and in prayer, we must first ask what "to believe" means. (*CCC #26*)

"I believe..." What could we possibly say about these two little words?
What does it mean to say "I believe?" Are there not many things we can
believe in? Is believing just some personal choice to believe in something
that makes us *feel better* about ourselves? Do we simply feel more secure
if we choose to believe in something greater than ourselves?

And what about the question of "Why?" Why do I believe what I do? Is
it just because this is what I was taught as a child? Is it simply because I
have no reason not to believe what I was taught?

Throughout history there have been countless people who have tackled
these questions. Some were among the most brilliant minds this world
has known. Others have exercised very little intellectual power. But it's
true that the countless masses of people throughout history have
pondered the question of belief. Some have done it in a very public way
through books and articles. Some have discussed these matters at home
with a spouse, children or friends. And others have kept these questions
inside pondering them for themselves not sharing their reflections for
fear of judgment or criticism.

What has your journey of belief looked like? Have you looked deeply at
the question of your beliefs? Do you even know what you believe? Have
you tackled the tough questions of God, the creation of the Universe,
the afterlife, the moral life, worship and the like?

If you've pondered these questions and come to some sort of conclusion, then have you also looked deeply at that second question of "Why?" Why do I believe this or that? Do I have a good reason for my beliefs? Or am I embarrassed or fearful to take a stand and make my convictions known?

The goal of this book is to address these questions head on. And it's essential that we look at this question of belief as a question first. In other words, unless we understand the question, and all the subsequent questions that go hand and hand with that question, we will never be able to properly come to the right answer. The true answer. The answer we truly believe and are willing to stake our lives on. But unless we've walked through the question properly, done our due diligence, explored all possibilities, and sought out the truth, then we will have a very hard time saying, with any real conviction, those two little words... "I believe!"

This chapter deals with faith, belief and the process of coming to faith and certainty. Take your time in reflecting upon it and don't move on until you've properly done your part. This is not only an intellectual exercise, it's also an exercise in openness to the Truth. It's an exercise in engaging the truth as it is, letting it sink in and letting it transform your life.

Let's begin by looking at the most fundamental desire there is.

The Desire for Happiness

There is one thing you cannot remove from your heart's desire. One thing you can never shake. One thing that you will always want and seek. In fact, this one thing is one of the most fundamental and guiding desires of your life and has an effect upon everything you do! What is this "one thing?" It's the deep and unshakable desire for happiness written upon the very depth of your being!

You want to be happy! Period. You can't shake that desire. Interestingly, even a life of the worst of sins is focused on the desire for happiness. Sure, when sin is chosen as a path to "happiness," there is confusion present. But nonetheless, even sin is done with a desire for happiness of some sort.

Take some examples: Why would someone use drugs? Because they have a false sense that this will make them happy. Or why does someone lose their temper and blow up in anger? Because they have a false sense that this venting of their anger will satisfy them. And, yes, in a twisted way it does temporarily satisfy. But the satisfaction with this and every sin is fleeting and ultimately leaves one less happy and more dissatisfied in life.

But the point here is the desire for happiness. It's unshakable. No one can honestly say, "I truly want to be miserable!" Some people make themselves miserable, but no one truly desires this. They just go about seeking happiness in the wrong way.

This desire for happiness is unshakable because it's a desire written upon our very nature. It's there, and it's not going away. By analogy, we can say "The sun is bright" or "Water is wet." "Brightness" and "wetness" are essential attributes of the sun and water. You cannot take them away. There is no such thing as a dull sun or dry water. Sure the sun may be covered with clouds or water may evaporate, but this doesn't change the very essence of what the sun or water is.

So it is with our human nature. An essential aspect of human nature is the desire for happiness. Humans want happiness, and there is no way to remove this desire from your heart. It may get covered up through sin or confusion or depression or despair. But deep down, the desire remains as an essential and integral part of our nature. It makes up part of who you are.

Tapping into and understanding this reality is key to understanding who we are and what life is all about. If the desire for happiness is part of our human nature, then the next obvious question deals with: "Fulfilling that Desire."

Fulfilling that Desire

So, if I come to a point where I agree that I desire happiness and that everything I do in life is, in some way, done with this desire as a directing principle, then the next question is quite obvious: "What is it that actually fulfills this desire and actually makes me happy?"

Good question. And perhaps intelligent minds will disagree on the answer to that. But a basic philosophical truth is that two things that contradict each other cannot both be true. For example, something cannot be both hot and cold at the same time, or black and white at the same time. Sure, one person may say their soup is hot while another may think the same soup is only warm. So there is a certain perspective involved. But ultimately the principle remains that two things that contradict each other cannot both be true.

The point is this—human nature is created and designed in such a way that there are in fact certain things that make us happy and certain things that make us miserable. And perhaps there are many things in between. But it's just not logical or rational to say that if one thing makes me happy, it will also make someone else miserable.

Now I know what you're thinking. You may be thinking that, for example, your spouse loves to go shopping and you are miserable shopping. Or you love to watch football but your friend hates football. What we have to understand is that some things create a more superficial "happiness" and others produce a more substantial and essential happiness. So, yes, football may be "fun" for one person and not for another. Or shopping, knitting, swimming, etc., may make one person excited and not another. But when we speak of the desire for "happiness," we cannot just settle for this more superficial level of things that are only entertaining or fun. We are not speaking of hobbies, pastimes or preferences. Rather, when we speak of that deeply ingrained desire for happiness, we are speaking of a whole different category.

So what is this other category? It's the category of love. For example, no one can truly say, "I hate to love and be loved." Sure, they can say that and even believe it, but, in reality, no one can love to hate or hate to love. Love is what we are made for. It's intertwined so deeply within us that it cannot be shaken. Deep down, we all love to love and to be loved.

The word "love" is a dangerous word to use here because in our culture it is so often misused and abused. Our concept of love has been skewed and distorted from its true divine meaning. So, the real answer is that the love that God designed and instituted is the ultimate source of our happiness and fulfillment. Therefore, we need to shed the cultural influences about what love is and try to arrive at the real meaning. What does God think about "love?" What is His definition? The answer to this question is the answer to our happiness.

Divinely designed love takes on many forms but always retains a true selflessness, sacrificial giving, freedom and totality. It can be found in the relationship of spouses, with children, among siblings, between friends and even with a stranger. In every relationship, love will take on a unique form but ultimately will mirror and share in the one love of God.

Ultimately, it is love that draws us into a deeper relationship with God. Love of God is what we were made for. This is happiness! And this is fulfillment! This is the only way to fill that longing in our heart and the only way we will address the desire that we cannot shake—love of God directly in our relationship with Him, and love of God by our giving and receiving love with those around us. When we understand this and begin to live it, then we have begun to understand this unshakable part of who we are.

Coming to Know God

If we are to love God, we must come to know Him. We cannot love someone we do not know. So how do we do this? How do we come to know God?

There are two basic ways. Both ways bring us to knowledge of God, but the second way brings us much deeper into our personal knowledge of Him and is necessary for a true relationship with Him. Below are the two ways.

First, we come to know there is a God simply by natural deduction. In other words, our brains can figure it out by a process of reasoning. It just makes sense! As you will see, our natural reasoning process toward a God cannot help us arrive at the full picture of the Christian God we love and worship. But it can give us a start and point us in the right direction. Let's start by looking at how this makes sense from the point of view of creation itself. There are several ways we can look at this, but we'll just look at it from a couple of them. This may seem overly philosophical, but it's important to understand nonetheless.

One way to look at it is to realize that the Universe must have had a beginning. There was a beginning to time. How do we know this? Because it doesn't make sense to say that the Universe simply always was with no beginning. Why? Because time moves in one direction. Forward. We can certainly imagine that time could go on (forward) infinitely. It's rational to think that there could be no end to time. But what about the reverse? Is it rational to think that time could have what philosophers call an "infinite regress?" That is, a day before yesterday, and a day before that, and a day before that...on and on and into infinity backwards? If you think too hard about this, your brain may hurt. It's hard to comprehend this possibility and ultimately does not seem possible. So what's the answer? The logical answer is that the Universe had to have a definite beginning. A starting point. But this begs the question, "How did it start?" And that's where we get our answer. There must be a power that is capable of starting the Universe, creating it, setting it into motion, and doing this out of nothing. Some scientists call this the Big Bang. But we will call it God.

Another way to look at this question of proving God's existence from a rational point of view is the reality of non-material "things." What are those things? They are beauty, love, free will, intelligence, and the like. The *Catechism* (#32) quotes Saint Augustine as he says:

Question the beauty of the earth, question the beauty of the sea, question the beauty of the air distending and diffusing itself, question the beauty of the sky... question all these realities. All respond: "See, we are beautiful." Their beauty is a profession [confessio]. These beauties are subject to change. Who made them if not the Beautiful One [Pulcher] who is not subject to change? (St. Augustine, *Sermo* 241, 2: PL 38, 1134)

Beauty is something real. We see it, understand it when we are faced with it, and somehow it reveals the Most Beautiful One. We also see within our self the reality of our interior life. We realize we have free will. An ability to know, love, communicate, cherish. We recognize our comprehension of moral goodness, concern and care. These and so many other human qualities are so much more than the result of a bunch of molecules acting within our physical bodies. We just know that. These qualities must come from somewhere, and that "somewhere" must be something spiritual. It must be more than physical. The acknowledgement of this brings us to the realization that there is something more than just the physical world. And the origin of this is what we call God.

When we really wrap our minds around this and are honest with ourselves, we realize that we can only scratch the surface of what this all means through our human reason alone. We can come to a point where we realize there is more. That there must be a source of all we are, all we know, and all we experience. But human reason cannot go much further. And human language is also insufficient in expressing this. But we do our best realizing that we are striving for that which we can only begin to fathom.

Our next step is to go beyond what our brains can figure out and turn to what we call revelation.

Revelation

So, if I were a philosopher and wanted to prove that God existed, I could prove certain things such as the fact that there must be a first cause of the Universe. And I could argue that the non-physical aspects of humanity, such as truth, beauty, knowledge, free-will, etc., must come from some source other than the physical makeup of my body. But it's hard to go beyond these points just from a logical argument. Therefore, if we want more, if we want to come to the understanding of who God is and how He has acted and continues to act in our lives, then we need more. So what is that "more?"

That "more" is *revelation*. Revelation is real. It's almost like a sixth sense. A spiritual sense. It's the way God speaks to us and personally convinces us of His divine nature. It's His personal love and care for us and His activity in our lives throughout history.

Revelation is both a public act on God's part but also a very personal act on His part. It's God Himself speaking, explaining, and acting within our lives. It's a personal communication with us and more! It's more in the real sense that God not only speaks to us in revelation but also calls us to know Him, understand Him, believe in Him, love Him, follow Him, and live united with Him. It's a true communion of love, a true relationship of love and the beginning of a complete transformation of our lives.

So how is it that God reveals Himself to us through revelation?

God Reveals Himself

When God speaks, we must listen. If we believe that, then it begs the question, "How does God speak so that I may listen?" As Scripture says, God speaks "In many and various ways..." (Hb 1:1–2). What are those many and various ways?

To answer this properly, we have to go back to the very beginning of time. We have to trace God's action and communication with humanity from the very beginning. So we start with Creation itself.

The Bible is the source of our knowledge of God speaking to us throughout history. It records God's activity in the lives of His people throughout time. But the Bible is much more than this, too! The Bible is a "Living Word," meaning, as we read the Bible, we actually encounter the Living God! We meet Him, and He reveals Himself to us. So let's see how this happens.

First, the Bible tells us how God spoke in the beginning of time creating the Universe and all that is within it. From there, we hear of Noah, Abraham, the patriarchs and prophets. And, of course, the Bible culminates with God speaking through His only Son.

Reading about all of this is not only like reading a history book; rather, we actually meet God Himself as we engage His Word. So, for example, when we read the story of creation, we learn about what God did and why He did it, but we also come to actually "know" God Himself! When we listen to the promises made to Noah and Abraham and listen to His words spoken through the prophets and patriarchs, we encounter a living God who loves us, has spoken to us and continues to speak to us today. And most especially, when we read the life of Jesus, listen to His words, and ponder His actions, we meet Him personally within those words. So the Bible is alive! It's an encounter with the Living God! And it's the instrument by which we establish our relationship with this loving and personal God.

God keeps speaking! He is not finished. Though everything He had to say is revealed in the Scriptures, and in the Person of His divine Son Jesus, He continues to reveal all He spoke by continuing that conversation within the Church today. So let's see how.

God Keeps Speaking

Yes, the Bible is the inspired Word of God and is the source of our knowledge of Him. But God takes that glorious source of revelation and continues to deepen our understanding of it through the Church. He gave the "Keys of the Kingdom" to Saint Peter and to all of his successors. They are entrusted with the responsibility of taking that revelation and making it present in every day and age. Every day and age has its own unique questions and concerns. That is why the Church is the *living* and *ever-present* source of God's continual voice. Again, He is alive today. He speaks today. He is alive in the Bible but also in the Church. We call this continual communication within the Church "Tradition."

Tradition is not just traditions. It's not just ideas or practices that have been passed on from age to age. It's not just customs or cultural practices. Tradition is the actual Living Word of God alive in each generation. Its foundation is the Bible, the foundational revelation of the Living Word of God, and its voice is the Church today and yesterday acting as an instrument, transmitting the Living Word.

How does this transmission work? It works through the Magisterium.

Magisterium

> "The task of giving an authentic interpretation of the Word of God, whether in its written form or in the form of Tradition, has been entrusted to the living, teaching office of the Church alone. Its authority in this matter is exercised in the name of Jesus Christ" (DV 10 § 2.). (*CCC* #85)

"Authentic interpretation of the Word of God?" Whose job is that? It's the responsibility of the Church in every day and age. But it is uniquely the responsibility of one part of the Church: The Magisterium.

Now, to some, the idea of the "Magisterium" and "authentic interpretation" may seem dry or even impersonal. It's similar to our relationship to the Supreme Court or the President in the secular world. Sure, we know they are important and we know they have a big influence upon society, but do they really affect me and my life? Well, yes, more than we realize. And so it is with the Magisterium, but in a way that is even "more real," so to speak.

The most important responsibility the Magisterium has in teaching is to define what we call dogmas. These are the Church's highest teachings. These teachings, and really all the teachings of the Church, have a very direct impact upon our spiritual lives. For example, if you pray the rosary, have a devotion to our Blessed Mother, have a devotion to the Blessed Sacrament, go to Confession, etc., then the Magisterium has had a very direct impact upon your life! You see, doctrine and dogma affect our personal life of faith more than we could ever realize. Why? Because it presents a transmission of the very Word of God for our day and age. And that Word is the path to our relationship with God.

Next, let's look more specifically at Sacred Scripture itself.

Sacred Scripture

The Scriptures are the inspired Word of God. But they are also the work of man. However, it's not a 50/50 project. Rather, we say they are 100% the work of the human author and 100% the inspired work of the Holy Spirit. So it's a 100/100 project!

This is clearly seen in the fact that each book is unique. Why are they unique? Because each book uniquely reflects the way the Holy Spirit shines through that particular chosen author. So Saint Paul writes in one unique way, and you can see his human personality shine through. Each Gospel is unique and reflects both the author and the community for which it was written. Saint John's Gospel, for example, is exceptionally unique from the others and clearly reveals God shining through his very humanity. But each part of the Bible is also 100% the inspired work of the Holy Spirit!

The Old and New Testament together make up one complete and total Testament of God's inspired Word. Each book was written at a different period in time and together reveal the unfolding mystery of God's activity in human history. Early on, as the books of the Old Testament were compiled, we see how God slowly prepared humanity for the coming of His Son. The Old Testament reveals the work of Creation, the fall of humanity, God's continual attempts to establish a new covenant, man's continual turning away from God, the role of the prophets, kings, Old Testament priesthood, sacrifices, prayers and much more. In the end, it all points to the New Testament when we discover Jesus fulfilling everything promised by God and prefigured in the Old Testament.

The New Testament was written over several decades and then was used by the early Church in its liturgies and teaching. Over the first several centuries of the Church, the question of which books and letters really were inspired was clarified and defined by various councils within the Church. A council is a gathering of the bishops for the purpose of teaching. The final and clearest statement from a council took place in the mid-sixteenth century, at the Council of Trent. At that council, the fathers clarified the definitive listing of the books of the Bible. It was definitively taught there that "the Church accepts and venerates as inspired the 46 books of the Old Testament and the 27 books of the New" (*CCC* #138).

One of the best things you can do is learn the Scriptures. Study them, read them and, most importantly, pray with them. As you do this, you will realize that the Scriptures are very much alive! As we enter into the Scriptures, we will be called to experience the gift that the Church has called the "Obedience of Faith."

Obedience of Faith

Here comes the "I" part of our reflection. Faith is both personal and public. It's public in that it's God's Word sent forth for all. It's the revelation given by God in the Scriptures and deepened throughout the ages by the Magisterium (Sacred Tradition). But the ultimate goal is our own personal conversion and faith.

When the public faith of the Church meets us in our consciences, we are called to encounter the Living God and meet, love, and come to know God Himself. This personal meeting calls for a completely free response on our part. It means we must see God and freely choose to believe in Him, love Him and surrender to Him. This produces the glorious gift of faith in our lives when we become "obedient" to the Voice of God out of love and by our own free will.

Though this is a free and personal choice on our part, it must also be an act of the Holy Spirit because, truth be told, we cannot come to faith on our own. Perhaps, by analogy, it would be like an infant eating baby food. The infant cannot open the jar, spoon out the food and feed himself. So it is with us. We must do the "chewing" so to speak, but it must be the Holy Spirit Who does the "feeding."

As we receive the gift of faith, we will slowly discover that it profoundly affects us in various ways. Here are some of those ways:

Faith is certain: How often are you certain about something? What if you could be certain about your future? Or, more trivially, what if you could be certain about who would win the next Super Bowl? Or what if you were certain about tomorrow's lotto numbers? Certainty changes things! It affects the decisions we make. It affects the direction we take in life. And conversely, uncertainty also affects us. It makes our decisions more difficult and our future more unstable.

Well, faith is one of those gifts that brings certainty to a whole new level. Sometimes we fall into the trap of thinking that faith is just a strong wish and hope with our fingers crossed. But it's not that at all! Faith, when it's true faith, is certain. It means we know. And we know on a level so deep that it does, indeed, affect everything we do and all the decisions we make as we move into the future. This certainty is something that only the Holy Spirit can give us. It's God speaking in His unique language through that spiritual sense He has implanted within us. And when it is His voice speaking, and our soul hearing, we are given a certainty beyond human conviction, which will direct all our actions.

Faith seeks understanding: The more we know, the more we want to know. We see this principle at work in many ways. In a distorted way, we are all aware of things like greed, or addiction, or lust. When one gains a little of these, the tendency is to seek more. That's because these disorders are simply acting upon the natural design of our human nature to want more. But that natural design was made to want more of God! And only when we use this desire for more of God are we functioning in the way we were made. So with faith we see this at work. The more one knows God, personally, truly, intimately, the more one wants to know God, love God and be with God all the more. And there is no limit to how much the human soul can receive of this glorious Gift! So seek God and let the gift of His presence in your life stir up the desire for more.

Faith and science: There are those who seem to think that faith and science are opposed. But are they? Most certainly not. Faith and science come from the same source, from the same designer, and they are 100% compatible with each other. In fact, the word "compatible" is almost insufficient to use. It's more like they are perfectly married, united, and in union. The laws of nature and the laws of grace come from God, and the more one honestly studies and understands the laws of nature (science), the more one is drawn into the deeper laws of grace. It's a "marriage" similar to the unity of our body and soul that we will reflect upon in the next chapter. So make a mental note to think about the unity of faith and science when you read the section on the unity of body and soul.

Freedom and faith: There is a key aspect of authentic faith that must be understood because at times it is greatly abused. This key aspect of faith is *freedom*. Unless a person is completely free in their cooperation with grace, they will never have authentic faith. Let's look at the danger involved here to illustrate the point. A great illustration is what we call proselytism. Specifically, I would distinguish proselytism from true evangelization. What is proselytism? It would be a forceful and manipulative way of convincing someone to be a Christian. For example, say a preacher preaches "fire and brimstone" and leaves a person so fearful of damnation that they "choose" to say they believe. Or, if someone imposes so much guilt on another for a choice they make that they "change," just because they don't want to deal with the guilt. This may be a small step in the right direction. But if it is, it's a very small step. And in fact, it may actually be a step backwards without us even realizing it.

What I mean is that for conversion and faith to happen, a person needs to be invited into the gift of faith freely for the sake of love. Sure, there is an authentic form of holy fear we should have, but ultimately the source of true faith is the *free choice* of the individual to believe *because* they believe, and to believe because it was the Holy Spirit speaking to their soul revealing the truths of faith, and inviting an authentic assent. Sound difficult? Well, God knows what He's doing. For our part, we just need to respect the way He passes on faith, and we will be more deeply converted and be a good instrument of that gift of faith for others.

Authentic faith is necessary for salvation, gives us strength to persevere, and is the beginning of eternal life. Faith is belief not so much in some philosophical principle; rather, faith is a belief in someone. It's a belief in what the Creed points to, the reality behind the words.

We conclude our reflections on faith but now turn to that which faith points. And it points to more than "something," it points to "Someone." And, of course, that "Someone" is God!

2

God and His Creation

One God

> God is unique; there is only one God: "The Christian faith confesses that God is one in nature, substance, and essence" (*Roman Catechism*, I. 2, 2.). (*CCC* #200)

The classic question is whether God is One or Three. The answer is "yes" to both. He is One and He is Three. One God, one nature, one substance, but three divine Persons. The best way to understand this is to understand it from the point of view of a family. Imagine a family in which there was perfect love and perfect unity. Of course, this is only possible in Heaven because we live in a fallen world. But just try to imagine it. A family where there is perfect love, perfect harmony, perfect unity, etc. Additionally, imagine if each individual were in perfect union with God's will. Each member knew, understood, chose and lived God's will perfectly. Now let's say this family is the Johnson family. You would say that this is one family but that this one family is made up of individual members. Different persons. But each person is a member of the one Johnson family, and that one family is perfect in every way.

Now I know a perfect family is close to impossible to imagine in this world. Even the best of families have regular disagreements and issues. But if you can try to imagine this ideal, then perhaps it's possible to at least understand the nature of God in an analogous way.

The analogy does fall short in one way. The Johnson family would be one family of many families in our world. But the family of the Trinity is the one and only divine family. The Trinity is the only family possessing divine nature. There are countless human families possessing human nature. So, consider the following points to help clarify:

The three Persons of the Trinity are the only three to share in the one divine nature.

–They love each other perfectly.

–They each have the same perfect knowledge of the Truth.

–They each share the same perfect will of love grounded in their perfect knowledge of the Truth.

Therefore, the three are of the same essence, nature and being. They are one while at the same time remain three.

There will be more to come on this in future reflections, but at least for now we are introduced to the concept.

God's Name

"But," said Moses to God, "if I go to the Israelites and say to them, 'The God of your ancestors has sent me to you,' and they ask me, 'What is his name?' what do I tell them?" God replied to Moses: I am who I am. Then he added: This is what you will tell the Israelites: I AM has sent me to you. (Ex 3:13–15)

How would you like to have the name, "I Am Who Am." Pretty deep. In fact, it's so deep that it's a name that can only be applied to God. This is God's name given Him by Himself and revealed to Moses for all to come to know. This is God's essence, His very being, His nature. It is Who He Is!

The *Catechism* explains this using mysterious language:

God is the fullness of Being and of every perfection, without origin and without end. All creatures receive all that they are and have from him; but he alone is his very being, and he is of himself everything that he is. (#213)

So what exactly does that mean? That's right! The question is the answer! Huh? Confusing? Well, in fact it's not actually confusing; rather, it's profoundly mysterious. This IS the nature and essence of God. To Be. To exist. To be existence itself. To have always been. And, interestingly,

God's name is a sort of refusal to have a name. It's as if God were saying, "Look, I cannot be named. My essence IS WHO I AM, and this is how I AM to be known."

Yes, it's still confusing. But that's OK. Perhaps what we should be happy understanding is that God cannot really be named, but if we try to do so, then we are left with a profound mystery. It's the mystery of His nature. And it will only be understood properly in Heaven. For now, though, we do our best.

What else can we say about God from His name? That He is stable, permanent, unchanging, the fullness and source of all being, the beginning and the end of all being, Truth and the source of all truth, and so much more. The rest of our reflections on the Creed should help us enter more deeply into this mystery of the essence and nature of God.

Now let's look more closely at God as Father.

Father

When we were baptized, we were baptized NOT in the names (plural) of the Father, Son and Holy Spirit. Rather, we were baptized in the name (singular) of the Father, Son and Holy Spirit. This Trinity is one. But God is also distinct in His Persons. So let's look at that.

Who is God the Father? Why do we call Him "Father?" Well, to begin, God the Father is neither male nor female. God the Father is eternally a pure Spirit. But an earthly father and mother both reflect various aspects of God. This shows that God the Father is, in fact, the source of all parenthood. The source of all begetting. The source of all that is. And He is not just the source of the physical world, not just the source of humanity, but is also the source of all that is good and beautiful in humanity. He's the source of love, tenderness, care, fidelity, authority, etc. God the Father is the source of all.

We should also realize that by calling God Father, Jesus reveals a very personal nature of this divine Person. THE Father is my Father, your Father, our Father. He is one Father. The only Father. The Father of all. But the key here is the personal nature of God. And it is the personal nature of a God who is our source, sustenance and sole support. Yes, it's mysterious also. No worries. Just do your best to understand what you can and remain open. Little by little, it will make sense.

Another question is specifically why we call Him "Him" and not IT or the Parent in Heaven? Because "Father" is the language Jesus used when revealing Him to us. Jesus called God the Father. So why did Jesus do this? Why did He use a male image? Not sure. We'll have to ask Him in Heaven. But this is the language He used, so it's the language we use. It's not a slap in the face in any way, shape or form to mothers. It doesn't lessen or cheapen the motherly role. It's simply what Jesus revealed and the language He used. But He used it for a reason. Perhaps, in part, it was because, in His eternal plan of salvation, we would have a new spiritual mother. We would be given the Mother of Jesus, the Mother of God as our mother. So, with Mary as our Mother and the Mother of all the Living, we also have God as our Father. No doubt this is not the only reason God is revealed to us as "Father," but it will suffice for now for our purposes.

God is not just "Father," He is also the "Almighty."

Almighty

Is there anything God cannot do? Is there anything beyond His power? He is called the one and only Omnipotent One. The All-Powerful One. So the answer is simple. No. Nothing is beyond the power of God.

"But wait a minute," you might say! Sure, it's easy to believe that God, the All-Powerful One created all things, sustains all things and could cause all things to cease to be in the blink of an eye. I understand that sort of power. But what about all the suffering in this world? Why is there so much suffering? And if God really is All-Powerful, and at the same time All-Loving, then why hasn't He fixed this? Why doesn't He just eliminate all suffering with a mere thought? If He is the All-Powerful One, couldn't He do this? Shouldn't He do this? Mustn't He do this?

Yes, He can do this, should do this and must do this if He is the All-Powerful and All-Loving One. But what you're missing if you ask this question is this: He already HAS done this! Sure, some may easily miss this point. We can look around and see people suffering. We see illness, the loss of loved ones, unjust persecution, tragedy and the like. This can lead us to conclude that God is distant and not exercising His Almighty Power! But He has exercised it and continues to exercise it in a way that is so deep, so profound, so mysterious and so perfect that it may easily go unnoticed when we ask this question. How has He exercised His Almighty Power in the face of the question of suffering? The Answer is Jesus, His divine Son. It was done by His suffering, death and resurrection. This is the answer the Father's perfect Almighty Power gave.

More will be said on this in the sections on Jesus' death and resurrection. But for now, suffice it to say that the Almighty gave the perfect answer to suffering in the Person of His Son. But before addressing this, let's stick with the nature and essence of the Father and ponder His act of creation by being the Maker of Heaven and Earth.

Maker of Heaven and Earth

One of the most fascinating topics of discussion for kids, believe it or not, is the creation of the Universe. As soon as they hear the story of Adam and Eve and then also learn about dinosaurs, their little minds begin to turn. "Did God create the dinosaurs?" they often ask. Kids are fascinated with questions and answers that surround the creation of the world, Adam and Eve, dinosaurs and cavemen, etc. But this topic is not just a fascination to kids! It also is something that those of all ages find curious.

So often one of the most puzzling questions that arises regarding the creation of the Universe revolves around the stories of Adam and Eve and also the seven days of creation. These are two different stories of creation. The problem is that they do not seem to be consistent with science. And they even appear to contradict each other. So what's the deal? What do we believe? Is there a true contradiction? Could the Bible have gotten it wrong? These are good questions deserving a careful and accurate answer.

First of all, it's important to point out that the two stories of Creation in the Bible are written using a specific literary style. They are not written as a science book is written. They are not intended to be a literal and factual telling of the creation of the world from a purely scientific approach. With that said, we must also say they are 100% true. True insofar as they clearly relate all that the sacred author and the Holy Spirit intended them to relate to us.

The purpose of these two stories is to reveal some basic truths of our faith. Here are some of those truths:

God is the Creator—God made all things out of nothing. This is a fact of our faith and also is completely consistent with all scientific data. Even science acknowledges the theory of the Big Bang as a very plausible idea for the creation of the world. The Big Bang supports the idea that there was a "time" before time. And then suddenly, for some reason still not fully understood to science alone, there was a "Bang!" A beginning, the start of motion, time, expansion...and the Universe began. The key here for our faith is that God is the origin and source of the Universe and created all things out of nothing.

Creation is a work of the whole Trinity—Though an understanding of the Father, Son and Holy Spirit was not explicitly revealed in the stories of creation, the Trinity is, nonetheless, seen and revealed in a mysterious way in the act of creation. God spoke and the Spirit hovered above the waters. This reveals the Father and the Spirit. And the fact that the Universe fell from its original state of innocence introduces the need for a Redeemer—God the Son. So the Trinity is introduced in a mysterious and hidden way even from the beginning of time.

God made the Universe to show forth His glory—Why did God create? Strictly speaking, He didn't have to. But He freely chose to in His Wisdom, and it resulted in the manifestation of His glory. We see the splendor of God in His creation, and we see God reflected in His creation. This is especially true of the creation of man.

The world is ordered and good—A key concept to understand from the creation stories is that the world is good and has a perfect order and design. This goodness is seen in all parts of the physical Universe. It's especially, once again, seen in the innate goodness of man.

The fall—By the free will of our human parents, disorder and sin were introduced into the world. This resulted in a fall of all creation from the state of original innocence which was God's original design. This fallenness affects all parts of God's creation and introduces the need for restoration and redemption. But the key here is that fallenness was not part of God's plan. It was the result of human free will.

So take the stories of Creation and the insights of science and blend them together so that we can gain a deeper understanding of the beginnings of time and the beginnings of the Universe. And, of course, the most important part of creation is the creation of Man.

Creation of Man in the *Imago Dei*—(Image of God)

We are made in the image and likeness of God. What does this mean? It means that of all of creation, man enjoys a unique and sacred quality not shared by the rest of creation. Only humanity is in the *imago dei*—the image of God. This is clearly seen in our understanding of what it means to be a person. No other living being, not dogs, cats, trees, or fish share in this gift of being a person.

What does it mean to be a person? Well, to understand this we have to first know who else is a person. There are three types of persons. There are human persons, angelic persons and divine persons. That is: humans, angels and God. The unique qualities that come with the dignity of being a person are the gift of an intellect and free will.

Now I know what some will say: "My dog has an intellect and will!" True, animals can "know" to a certain extent and can "will" to a certain extent. But their intellectual and willing capacity is of a far different nature than that of humans, angels and God. Only the latter three are capable of full self-knowledge, self-possession, sacrificial love and deep spiritual communion with each other. Animals are not capable of this.

They can know in the sense that they remember, can learn, and can act on instinct. They can even experience a certain level of emotion and feeling. But this does not mean that they are capable of truly "knowing" another. They cannot know and understand the nature of reality, comprehend the goodness of God and others, etc. And they cannot love for the sake of love. Freely giving of themselves in a true sacrificial way. They cannot give, in love, on the level of charity. And they cannot come to know and love God. Sorry dog lovers...it's just the way it is!

As a person, we, the angels and God are all capable of entering into a relationship of true communion with others through the exercise of our intellect and free will. It's this ability to be in communion, in relationship, that enables us to live our dignity and vocation. We are made for this communion, and, in fact, that is what Heaven ultimately is! It's an existence of perfect communion, unity and love united with God and all those others united to God. It's a relationship, a bond, and a oneness. This is what it ultimately means to be in the image and likeness of God. It's our capacity found in the dignity of being persons. Of course only God knows and loves perfectly. But that doesn't change the fact that we are still capable of both.

Next we look at the fact that one of man's most unique characteristics is that he unites the material and spiritual worlds in his person.

The Unity of Body and Soul

OK, so angels are pure spirits, but humans are both body and spirit. That can be confusing, but it's true. But a danger is to think that we, as humans, are only part body and part spirit. A 50/50 mixture. And what about when we die? Doesn't our body die but our spirit live on? So are we then angels? These are good questions that can be easily answered if we understand what it means to be human and how God created us.

To be human means we are 100% body and 100% spirit. And the two of those are not just two parts of who we are. Rather, these two qualities we have are fully united in such a way that, in philosophical language, we say *the soul is the form of the body*. The soul is created by God at the moment of our conception and joined to the body in such a way that the unity of these two make up the one human nature. So, interestingly, it is humanity which acts as a bridge between the material and spiritual worlds. The two worlds are united in us. And, of course, that is why the redemption of the world is united in Jesus.

It should also be pointed out that at times we speak of the soul as something distinct from the spirit. We also sometimes speak of the heart as something more than just physical. Various philosophers and theologians throughout time have used the terms in various ways. But suffice it to say that "soul," "spirit" and "heart" are all, for the most part, interchangeable referring to the immaterial aspects of our human nature.

From this understanding of the unity of body and soul, we move also to the unity of male and female.

Male and Female

Complementarity is the key! The fact that men and women are different is a fact so obvious that it usually evokes a smile when said out loud. Even children know this. Boys like to typically play one way and girls another. And they can perceive the difference.

The danger is that, at times, the differences between men and women have been abused and exaggerated to the point of undermining the intent and design of God for the opposite sexes. Some stereotypes would say that men can become "domineering" and "overpowering," while women can become "overly emotional" and "sensitive." When femininity or masculinity becomes distorted, then so does the possibility of mutual unity.

Just as we are made with a body and soul, and that body and soul form a single person, so also male and female are to be united and "become one." Not "one" in the sense that they are no longer two, or no longer individual persons, but one in the sense that they have the capacity of becoming united in a complementary way, being the ideal "helpmate" for the other. They form a bond in marriage that is inseparable and reflects and shares in the unity we are all called to share in with the Trinity.

The key point here, for this reflection, is to understand that humanity was designed and created by God as male and female. It's part of our nature. And it has a purpose that we must seek out, discover and live.

And this design was initially meant to be lived out in a state of original paradise.

Original Paradise

God created humanity with the intention of living in a perfect paradise of peace, harmony and union with God. This is the original "Heaven," so to speak. It is referred to in Genesis as the Garden of Eden.

In this place there would be nothing that accompanies our fallen nature. No illness, pain, suffering. No sin, discord or unhappiness. It would have been a physical place that Adam and Eve, our first parents, lived. It was a real place. In this place, there would have been no distortion of human nature. That means the effects of what we call "concupiscence" did not exist there. Concupiscence is the disorder we all experience within our soul that tempts us from acting contrary to our dignity. It's the distortion of our emotions, desires, our intellect and will. These struggles were not present in this original earthly paradise.

Later on we will see how the new Heaven, opened up by Jesus' life, death and resurrection, is a much better place than even this original paradise. But for now we need only acknowledge the original "state of holiness and justice" intended by God.

From there we have the sad reality of the fall of man.

The Fall of Man

Left to our own self-reflection, we cannot properly and fully understand and acknowledge the reality of sin. This especially applies to the reality of original sin but also applies to personal sin. We need divine revelation to shed light on it. But when it does, the picture becomes clear. Sin is real.

But the good news is that when we recognize the reality of sin, we also should realize the need for a Redeemer! More on this later. For now, let's look at sin.

Sin was first introduced into reality with the fall of the angels. The angels were created good as pure spirits possessing both an intellect and a will. With these two natural powers, of knowing and willing, they are capable of making decisions and acting on them. Their purpose is to know and love God freely, to know the greatness and glory of God, to acknowledge their role in the order of creation, and to freely will to live out their calling in love. This is what they are made for! But with the freedom to love, they also have the freedom to hate. And with the freedom to know God, they also have the freedom to reject the truth about God and themselves.

Their sin, then, was to reject the omnipotence of God and their relationship to Him out of pride. In this rejection, they also reject their role of loving humanity and serving out of love. This spiritual pride turned them from God, and thus they went forth exercising their spiritual angelic powers in opposition to the plan of God. Scripture says that one third of the angels fell. The leader of these angels, the highest of them, is the devil, or satan. His name is Lucifer, which means "light bearer." His original calling was to bear the light of God!

We see in the story of creation that satan was present exercising his angelic power of influence over Adam and Eve. As a fallen angel, he used this power of influence to lie and deceive. He led our first parents into believing that God was not Who He was and that they were more than who they were. He said to them that if they disobeyed God and ate of the forbidden fruit, they would "be like God."

As explained earlier, the question of whether the story of Adam and Eve actually happened literally, the way it is written, is not the point. That story teaches not so much literal, historical and scientific facts. Rather, it teaches the necessary truths of creation and the fall. So the story is true insofar as it teaches us that Adam and Eve, our first parents, gave into temptation and turned from God.

Some may think that it's not fair that we have to suffer the consequences of original sin just because our first parents turned from God. Here is a good way to understand this. Imagine that your parents moved to China before you were born. When you were born, you were born in China. It's not your doing but is a natural consequence of their choice. So it is with sin. When our first parents were cast out of paradise because of their sin, all their offspring are born into the state or condition they found themselves in. It's the natural consequence that affects us.

But there is no reason to lose hope! The fact of the matter is that, even from the first moments of sin, God's plan of redemption was put in place. The amazing thing is that God has willed to take our sin and transform it and our fallen condition in such a way that we are brought to an even higher place than our original state of innocence in the Garden. The promise of a redeemer, the Son of God taking on flesh, becoming human, uniting Himself to our nature, brings with it the unfathomable calling of God. We are now called to share in God's very life. The first insight into this is seen immediately in Genesis when there is this promise: "I will put enmity between you and the woman, and between your offspring and hers; He will strike at your head, while you strike at his heel" (Gn 3:15). In other words, the Savior is coming! And "the Woman" is clearly seen as a reference to our Blessed Mother. This is hope. The *Catechism* quotes Saint Thomas as saying, "God permits evil in order to draw forth some greater good," and Saint Paul is quoted as saying, "Where sin increased, grace abounded all the more" (#412). Yes, Romans 6:23 says, "The wages of sin is death..." but it then goes on to also say, "...but the Gift of God is eternal life in Christ Jesus our Lord!" Hold on to that hope in faith, and you will see the unlimited good God wills to bring even from the horror of our fallen state and our sin.

Of All Things Visible and Invisible

This line from the Creed is a clear reference to all we reflected upon in the previous section regarding God's creation and God Himself. It's a simple profession of the fact that reality consists of both that which is spiritual and material. God created the physical world out of nothing.

He also created the "invisible" world out of nothing which is a reference to the angels (and fallen angels) and our own spirits. And we also profess a belief in the existence of that which is not created but is invisible: Namely, the Most Blessed Trinity!

From here we look at the very person of Jesus Christ and His Mother.

3

The God-Man and His Mother

So who is Jesus Christ? Who is He who is our Lord and our God? Who is He who is our Savior and Redeemer? Who is He who is God from God and the Only Begotten? Who is He who is the Consubstantial One? Jesus takes on many titles. He is eternal. He is God. But He is also man. And this fact presents a great mystery to us. It also presents us with the reality of God's unfathomable love for us. So let's take a look at this God-man and try to understand who He is and what He has done for humanity. The truth of who Jesus is will shock us with a holy shock. It will leave us with a burning love for Him and gratitude that will compel us to give Him our lives. His life is, no doubt, the greatest story ever told!

Professing Faith in a Person

I believe in one Lord, Jesus Christ...

When we profess our faith in Christ, we are professing our faith in a person. It would be kind of like saying to someone, "I believe in you! I know you can do this or that. I know your goodness and believe this can shine through, etc." Believing in someone is a profession that this or that person has potential for good. We see that, acknowledge it, and profess it as true. Well, though this does get at the heart of our profession in Christ, we do need to add some important nuances so as not to be misled.

First of all, believing in Christ is not so much a favor we do for Him, rather, it's a favor He does for us. Our profession comes about because the public revelation of "Who He is" also becomes personal and real. God reveals the truth of His very Person to us in our conscience, and we accept that revelation as true. So this personal faith is a gift and a realization of the truth.

Second, our act of faith is also an act of love. To profess the truth of who God is in the Person of Jesus Christ is also to love Him. When we truly know Him and believe in Him, we are compelled to love Him and cooperate fully with His plan of redemption. We cannot fully comprehend Him and then fail to love Him at the same time. A lack of love also implies a lack of understanding. The two go hand in hand.

Third, knowing and loving Him changes us, it doesn't change Him. God is immovable and unchanging. But we are always changing insofar as we are drawn deeper into either the Truth or error. The more we come to know Christ the more we are changed by the Truth and become more fully human, more fully who we are made to be. And, conversely, the more we lack knowledge of Christ, the more we become less human, less of who we are. So the often quoted phrase from John 8:32 "...the Truth will set you free" applies here. Knowing Christ, He who is the Truth, the Lord, the Son, frees us to be who we are. So let's look at who He is.

Jesus, Christ, Son & Lord

Let's take a moment to look at the more technical aspects of who Jesus is, what His name means and what His titles mean.

Jesus means in Hebrew: "God saves." (*CCC* #430)

This phrase tells us not only who Jesus is—God—it also tells us what His mission is—to save! As the people of the Old Testament continued to progress in an understanding of themselves and God's interaction in their lives, they slowly understood, on a deeper and deeper level, the reality of sin. The good news was that with a greater understanding of the reality of sin, they understood more and more the need they had for a Savior. Jesus becomes that promised Savior. And the name Jesus itself is now sacred and powerful and evoked in prayer. Simply to call on the name of Jesus is to pray. There is power in the name of Jesus! One day all will bend a knee as this name is proclaimed!

> The word "Christ" comes from the Greek translation of the Hebrew Messiah, which means "anointed." (*CCC* #436)

Just as a king or a prophet is anointed for his mission, so also is the Christ. He is anointed by the Father with the Spirit. In His very anointing, we see the full action of the Trinity.

> Only in the Paschal mystery can the believer give the title "Son of God" its full meaning. (*CCC* #444)

Jesus' title as "Son" is spoken numerous times by numerous people in the Gospels. This title is also used at times in the Old Testament. It refers to Him being eternal, existing before the Universe, always in this unique relationship to the Father. It also reveals the intimacy between the Father and the Son. Jesus is the "Beloved Son." The relationship within the Trinity is one that is deep and personal. It is a relationship that reveals a familial bond.

He is also called the "Only Begotten" Son. This implies that He is the one and only of His kind. There are no others like Him. Sure, we are all sons and daughters of God, but we are called "adopted" children of God. Jesus is the only one "born" of the Father. This again shows His unique relationship with the Father and shows that He, and He alone, shares in the very nature of the Father. He is God. He is Light from Light. He is True God from True God. He is Begotten and not made. In other words, He is the only one of His kind and holds a very special and unique relationship with the Father. That relationship must always be honored, adored, acknowledged, and identified as one of a kind. The Creed also calls Him "Consubstantial" with the Father. This is a philosophical term stating, once again, that He is also God. He is of the same divine "substance" as the Father.

> The New Testament uses this full sense of the title "Lord" both for the Father and—what is new—for Jesus, who is thereby recognized as God Himself (Cf. 1 Cor. 2:8). (*CCC* #446)

The title of "Lord" is used often for Jesus. It's a title of great respect. But it is also a title used for the Father. Because "Lord" is used for both

Jesus and the Father, it points to the divinity of Jesus, just as the Father is divine.

Through Him All Things Were Made (John 1:3)

This line is quite simple in its meaning, while at the same time it is quite profound and mysterious. First, it shows that the Trinity acts in unity. Everything the Father does is also done in union with the Son. They act as one. Their will is one. Yet they are still distinct in their Persons. But the key here is their unity of action. The created world is an act of God the Father, through the Son, by the power of the Holy Spirit. It's simple, yet it is also mysterious. This leads us to a second point.

The act of creation cannot be fully understood and comprehended by us. It is beyond us. It is glorious, real, an act of God, but mysterious at the same time. A mystery is not so much something that we cannot figure out. Rather, a mystery in Christian language is something we are called to enter into on a deeper and deeper level all the time. And so it is with the act of creation. God, in His omnipotent power, was able to create all things. Ponder this simple truth of faith and let it sink in deeper as you do.

One of the greatest mysteries of God is the act of the Incarnation. The Incarnation is the fact that God took on our nature. He took on the nature He created. So let's now look at this mystery of Him coming "down from Heaven."

God Becomes Man—Why He Did It

For us men and for our salvation he came down from heaven...

Why did God become a human being? We are so used to the story that we may miss this important question. And if we miss the question, we may also miss the answer. Couldn't He have saved us another way? Did He really have to be born of the Virgin Mary? Did He have to become a little child? A poor child? Be raised like any other child? Learn to walk and talk? Grow and mature? Did He really have to become one of us sharing all parts of our life?

The proper answer is both "yes" and "no." "No" in the sense that God can do whatever He wills. He could have chosen a different way to redemption. But He didn't. So, for that reason, we shouldn't even ask the question of whether or not He could have chosen to redeem us a different way. Reality is reality, and things are the way they are. And that's that.

The answer is also "yes." Yes, God had to become one of us simply because this is His divine will and the way things are. So we should accept this fact as a fact and try to understand not so much "why," rather, we should seek to understand what the results are of Him becoming man.

God Becomes Man—What He Did

So what are the results of God becoming man? What does this do to and for us? How are our lives affected by this act? These are profoundly significant questions.

First, we can say that God becoming man—the Incarnation—reconciles us to the Father. In other words, there was a problem. Something was broken. We were not at peace and harmony with the Father. And this had to be fixed. So when Jesus took on our human nature, there was suddenly a reunion of sorts with God. Jesus is God and also man. Since He is God, He is fully united with the Father. And His humanity was fully united to His divinity. Therefore, the effect was that humanity itself, that is, human nature itself was able to be reunited to the Father. Now read that paragraph again slowly to make sure you followed it. It takes a little extra concentration.

This also means that we, in our human nature, can experience all that Jesus experienced in His human nature. And one of those experiences was the love of the Father. So we can now experience this love again because of the bridge that was made between God and humanity in the very Person of Jesus. This unity is potentially so complete that we are able to actually share in God's divinity. This is mysterious to say but true. We do not actually become divine, but we do share in God's divine life.

Jesus is also our perfect model. No, He's not _only_ a role model for us, He is so much more. But He is a role model nonetheless. He's an example and model for our holiness and unity with the Father. We look to Him to know how to live and to understand what we are called to as humans. He is the perfect human and, therefore, the perfect example.

100/100—Fully God and Fully Human

Jesus is not part God and part human. He's not like one of the Greek gods who has a human mother and divine father. Rather, He takes on both natures 100%. This concept is similar to the understanding outlined earlier that Scripture is 100% inspired by God and 100% the work of the human author. It's also similar to the understanding that human beings are a full unity of body and soul.

Jesus was always God. God the Son existed from eternity. He was not created at the moment He became human. Our souls, however, _are_ created in that moment. We are not eternal. We may be everlasting in that we will always exist from now on. But we are not eternal in that we do have a definite beginning. Jesus is different. He is eternally God and, as God, has no beginning. But at one moment in human history, He took on this new nature, the human nature. He is the only one to ever do this, and this is what we call the Incarnation.

In our earlier reflection on the human soul, we looked at the philosophical fact that our body and soul are united in our person. We are one person comprised of body and soul. So it is with Jesus. He is one Person, the Eternal Son of God. And that Person also assumes His human nature. He is not two but is one. The unity of His human body and divine soul are perfect and are one. Again, it's mysterious language we use, but that shouldn't keep us from using it.

Within that body and soul, we look at another mystery. Jesus has two wills—a human will and divine will. But, with that said, it must also be mysteriously said that they are united as one. They do not oppose each other or fight each other. They are united in Him and act as one. And the ultimate way that this unity of wills was made manifest for the world to see was His free embrace and willing acceptance of the will of the Father to embrace the Cross.

Lastly, we should point out that Jesus' heart was truly human and truly divine. This is an AMAZING reality to ponder. It means that a human being is capable of loving like God. A human loves with the love of God. The heart of God is alive in human nature. Again, wow! This is extraordinary and so very significant for all humans. It shows us the potential we now have for love. It's an infinite potential, and we are all called to share in it!

Now we turn to our Blessed Mother and reflect upon her and her role in Salvation.

God's Perfect Plan

...and by the Holy Spirit was incarnate of the Virgin Mary, and became man.

It was the Holy Spirit who overshadowed the Blessed Virgin Mary inviting her participation in the act of the Incarnation. The incarnation is the moment in time when God, the eternal Son, took on flesh in the womb of Mary. This was not done through the marital act, rather, it was done by an overshadowing of the Holy Spirit. This is the beginning of the "fullness of time" in that God is now united with humanity in a new and profound way.

Mary was the chosen one for this mission from all eternity. It was eternally the will of God to bring this act forth in and through her. But she had to be a willing participant. Eve had said "no" to God by her disobedience and, thus, humanity suffered the consequences. Mary enabled humanity to enter into this new relationship with God by her "yes." By her free choice of obedience, the Savior came.

Mary's Immaculate Conception

God prepared our Blessed Mother for this by a special grace. We call it a "prevenient grace." She was preserved from the effects of original sin from the moment of her conception. We call this the "Immaculate Conception." In this preservation God applied the redeeming power of Christ her Son *retroactively*. How did God do this? Not sure. But He did it; and since He is God, He obviously knows what He's doing and how to do this. God transcends time, so He can act outside of time—and that's what He did. He took the saving power of His Son's life, death and resurrection and transmitted this to the Blessed Virgin at the moment of her conception. Thus, her Son was her Savior and He saved her even before He was born. What a wonderful mystery of faith to ponder!

This grace of the Immaculate Conception certainly had dramatic effects on Mary. But what's important to note is that this preservation she received at the moment of her conception did not make her less human. Rather, it made her more human in a sense. In other words, it's commonly said that "to sin is to be human." But that's not true. Sin is not, properly speaking, something that is essentially part of who we are. In fact, the contrary is true. To sin is actually to act contrary to our humanity and our dignity. Therefore, Mary is the only one, other than her Son, who acted always in accord with her human dignity. And her perfect cooperation with the eternal plan of God in the Incarnation is the perfect example of that fact. She didn't have to always act in obedience and love, but she did so by her own free will. Her perfect "yes" was an example of how she always lived throughout her life. In that "yes" she said, "Behold, I am the handmaid of the Lord. May it be done to me according to your word" (Lk 1:38).

Mother of God

Mary is given many titles, and among them the most sacred title is that of the "Mother of God." This title is given her because she bore the eternal Son as her own child. She is the God-bearer. This actually says just as much about Jesus as it does about Mary. Jesus is true God and true man. Since He is not divided within Himself, then Mary is the mother of this Person. And this Person is God as well as man. So if one were to say that Mary is only the mother of the flesh of the Son, this would be strange and inaccurate. A mother is the mother of a person, not a nature. Her Son is a Person, and this Person is God. Therefore, the logical and definitive conclusion is that Mary is the Mother of God.

The Virgin Mother

Scripture is quite clear that Mary conceived Jesus in a virginal way—by the Holy Spirit. Additionally, it is the constant teaching of the Church that she always retained her virginity. She had no other children and never engaged in the marital act with Joseph. Sometimes this is confusing since there are references in the Scriptures to Jesus' brothers and sisters. But this language was commonly used in reference to cousins. So this shouldn't confuse us if we understand the language of the time. In fact this is still a common practice in other cultures of our day. For example, those from various African countries commonly refer to those within their own village as their brother or sister when they are with them outside of that village.

It was God's plan that Mary only have one Son for various reasons. It was especially so because of the fact that we are all called to become brothers and sisters of Christ through spiritual adoption. Therefore, if Jesus had blood brothers or sisters, it would have undermined his spiritual brotherhood with them. It would have made their relationship with Jesus different. But God desires this deeper spiritual relationship with all people. Mary is the only blood relation to Jesus, thus, she shares a special bond with Him that no one else does. But it had to be that way if God was to become true man.

Interestingly, though, even Mary's deepest bond with Jesus does not come as a result of her physical blood relationship. It comes, first and foremost, by her spiritual motherhood. She is united with her Son primarily by her perfect faith and obedience. It is this bond that surpasses the natural one.

The Final Outcome

Mary undoes the sin of Eve and, thus, becomes the new Mother of all the Living. She is the new Eve in the order of grace. She, therefore, becomes our spiritual mother insofar as we are united with her Son. By becoming one with Jesus, we adopt His own Mother in this new family of man. And Jesus' perfect obedience makes Him the new Adam, the new Father of all the Living. So we are not only spiritual siblings of Jesus, He is also our father in the order of grace. And only in Him can we call the one Father in Heaven "Our Father."

Now that we've reflected upon Jesus as God and His Incarnation as man, let's look at His suffering and death.

4

God Suffers "Death"

The Paschal mystery of Christ's cross and Resurrection stands at the center of the Good News that the apostles, and the Church following them, are to proclaim to the world. (*CCC #571*)

Perhaps the most well-known fact of Jesus' life is that He was crucified. Or is it the most well-known fact? Sure, we are very familiar with the story, we see the crucifix hanging in our homes and churches, but do we really "know" the meaning and significance of this act? Do we really know what it is all about? Do we understand why Jesus had to suffer and die? Or do we easily gloss over this central fact and typically turn our eyes only to the Resurrection and God's presence in Heaven?

Certainly we must fully embrace the Resurrection of Christ and acknowledge His eternal presence in Heaven from where He continually ministers to us. But we should not overlook the significance of that real and historical event of His suffering and death. We should not miss its meaning, its power and its effect in our lives. Jesus died for a reason. And He died the kind of death He died for a reason. So let's ponder that reality and event for a while and see how significant it is in our lives.

To begin, let's start with Jesus' life leading up to His suffering and death for a little context.

Jesus Makes Some Enemies

How could someone who has perfect charity offend another? How could Jesus, the eternal Son of the Father, have people oppose Him and dislike Him to the point that they wanted Him dead? Sounds strange. It's easy for us to fall into the thinking that "If I'm just nice and loving, everyone will love me." But that was not the case with Jesus.

Love, to be true and authentic love, must be grounded in the truth. And sometimes the truth can hurt. The content of the truth can hurt someone's pride when they do not accept it, and the presentation of the truth can hurt someone's pride when they are faced with the truth presented with authority beyond their own. These were the challenges Jesus faced.

Jesus, along with the Father and the Holy Spirit, was obviously responsible for the entirety of the law which was handed down through the ages and was revealed by the great prophets. All of the Old Testament laws from God were just that...they were from God. But how they were interpreted left room for error and discord. The Pharisees and Sadducees were experts in the law and taught the people according to their own understanding and interpretation of it. And then along comes Jesus. He takes the law, as well as all prophecies of the Old Testament, and gives them a definitive and authoritative interpretation. Ouch! This was too much for many of the religious teachers of that time to handle! Who did Jesus think He was? Who gave Him the interpretations He was teaching? Where did His deep conviction come from?

Human nature is such that the pride of the teachers of the law, in Jesus' day and age, was wounded when confronted by the mere presence of Jesus. They did not enjoy the "awe factor" Jesus did. People did not hang on their every word as they did with Jesus. This bothered them, and they got angry. They started to pick apart all that Jesus was teaching, and they tried to find fault with what He said. This created quite a conflict. Jesus, of course, was not backing down. He was not intentionally stirring things up, rather, He was just teaching the truth that people needed to hear, and He was doing it with great calm, conviction and clarity. And people responded. The Pharisees responded also. They responded by plotting against Him to stop Him. And, sadly, this was a result of their wounded pride.

At times, Jesus would teach something that was beyond the understanding of the Pharisees. For example, regarding the temple that Jesus greatly respected, He said, "Destroy this temple and in three days I will raise it up" (Jn 2:19). This was remembered and brought up at His trial as a blasphemy. But if you understand what Jesus was actually saying, then you'd realize He was prophesying the truth. He is the new temple and they would destroy Him, and He would rise up on the third day. So there were statements Jesus made that were completely misunderstood but, nonetheless, were completely true.

At other times Jesus would take on the Scribes and Pharisees. "Woe to you, scribes and Pharisees, you hypocrites..." He went on to call them "blind guides" and "blind fools" (Mt 23:15–17). Again, His statements were true. But they hurt. They hurt not because Jesus was too harsh or rude, they hurt because of the pride of those to whom these words were directed. In reality, this was an act of love on Jesus' part.

Another "scandal" Jesus caused was His love and tenderness toward the sinner. He ate with tax collectors. Prostitutes were following Him and listening to His every word. He ignored the proud and haughty and associated with the lowly and the sinner. This gave His enemies fuel for their fire.

And lastly, the most inflammatory thing Jesus did was to assume the identity of God. He forgave sins. He spoke of His works as the works of the Father. He identified Himself as "I AM." And He stated that "The Father and I are One." This was too much for them. It was all true, all beautifully true, but too much for them to believe and comprehend. And, again, it was especially because of their pride and their hardened hearts. All of this created enemies for Jesus and, in the end, it cost Him His life.

Who is Responsible for His Crucifixion?

Though Jesus had many who were against Him, He also had many who were for Him and were His followers. This included many ordinary people of His day, as well as some of the prominent Jewish leaders. So, as the plot against Jesus grew, it was not any one specific group or person who was responsible. Yes, there was a conspiracy within the Sanhedrin, Judas betrayed Him and Pilate made the final decision. But it would be a mistake to blame any one of them or any particular group. Why? Because Jesus gave His life willingly. It was part of the Father's permissive will that He die for all. So, in a sense, we can say that it was the Father's will that was behind this. But the Father willed this, by His permission, because there was a greater good. He knew that by allowing His Son to be crucified, that act of sacrificial love would triumph in the end. Ultimately, even though the Father permitted this act, it's only truthful to say that all who have sinned are guilty of shedding the blood of Christ. This act was permitted for the sake of the forgiveness of all sin; thus, everyone who has committed sin is guilty. That's us! True, we can make the claim that "I would never have participated or supported such a thing!" Perhaps. But it was still an act of love to wash away our sin that brought about Jesus' death, so we're still guilty.

Let me offer an analogy. Analogies are never perfect, but I think it sheds at least a little light on the dilemma. Let's say that there is a new drug on the market that cures a particular ailment that you have. It's the only drug that has been known to work, but it was manufactured through some process that is immoral. Is it possible to say, "I'm opposed to the process, but I'm going to buy the drug anyway?" No, not really. The fact of buying that drug makes you a cooperator in the immoral process of creating the drug. Again, this is not a perfect analogy, but it helps illustrate the main point. And the main point is simply that you cannot separate the remedy from the source. Jesus' death is the remedy, and we are sick. The evil of His crucifixion was the means of giving us the cure. So, the conclusion is that we are responsible for His crucifixion. We may love Him, worship Him and serve Him, but we are still responsible. And God is not only OK with that, He willingly invites us to receive the fruit of His suffering and death. But we are only being honest when we acknowledge the fact of our responsibility in and cooperation with His death.

The Havoc Caused by Disobedience

So what was accomplished by Jesus suffering as He did and dying on the Cross? Remember that He said to Peter at His arrest that He could have called on the myriads of angels in Heaven to come to His assistance at anytime. And they would have shown up and defended Him with the greatest of ease! But He didn't call on them. He allowed Himself to be arrested, ridiculed, mocked, tortured, beaten, condemned and crucified. And after all of that, He died a human death.

For most of His followers, this would have been devastating. They would have been utterly confused and, perhaps, even scandalized. Some immediately started to believe that they had been fooled, deceived, and misled. Jesus was dead, and He died a horrible death. How could this have been the Messiah?

Perhaps we have a hard time entering into this human drama and dilemma since we know the end of the story. We easily skip over the suffering and death, and we jump to the Resurrection. But it's essential that we ponder the suffering and death of Jesus fully and deeply if we are to also enter into an understanding of His Resurrection. So, again, why? Why did He do this? And what did it accomplish?

One of the most important pieces in understanding the answer to this question is to look at the original cause of sin: disobedience. Adam and Eve disobeyed God. And this disobedience brought about their fallen nature and ours. Disobedience to God is a way of saying "no" to His perfect plan. It's a way of telling God, "I'll do it my way!" But the problem with this is not so much that God gets angry at us and punishes us, rather, the problem is that God respects our decision and lets us do it our way. He does not impose His will and plan upon us. So the disobedience of our first parents sets them on their own journey, and the result is that they get lost. Lost trying to discover their own way and their own meaning of life. They enter into a fallen state which wreaks havoc on their lives. They can no longer see the way and choose the good. They no longer can clearly understand the voice of God and respond to Him. They are lost.

But God does not just give up on them or on us. We, too, experience this fallen and lost state. This is Original Sin. We suffer the loss of clarity and direction in life. We cannot find our way. The result is that we also sin and disobey God. And, once again, God respects our freedom and allows us to turn away as we so choose. The consequence of this, if we were not given a second chance, is that we would die an eternal death. We would never find our own way back to the Giver of Life. But, again, God does not give up on us. Here enters Jesus!

Free and Perfect Obedience Untangles Disobedience

So back to our original question, "What was accomplished by Jesus suffering as He did and dying on the Cross?" Perhaps an analogy here will help. Imagine you are a child and you want to go explore the nearby forest. You have been told numerous times by your parents not to go there, but you sneak away and go anyway, telling your sister not to tell mom and dad. You get into the forest and are amazed. You wander by oaks and pines, cross a creek, climb a few trees and enjoy a few hours there. Suddenly you notice it is getting dark, and you decide to return home. But all of a sudden you realize you have no idea which way is home! As you panic, you get lost in the middle of some thorn bushes and get even more frightened. After wandering in circles for an hour, it is pitch dark, the sounds of night come out, and you sit there crying and frightened.

So what's your best hope? Your parents. You hope they will rescue you. You hope your sister told them where you went, and you hope they are on their way. As you sit lost and hoping you see a flashlight in the distance, you hear your name being called. It's your dad. You are completely relieved to hear him and see him coming and are grateful you were found. You talk, and he quickly forgives you but explains that you'll be spending the night in the forest. But he quickly adds that he will be staying with you. It's too dark to find your way back now, so you'll have to wait till morning light. Fortunately, your dad anticipated this and brought with him two sleeping bags and some food. In the end, it turns out to be one of the most memorable nights of your life, thanks to your dad.

Now, as always, this analogy only gets at one part of the answer to the question of Jesus' suffering and death. The fact is that we were completely lost and could not find our way home. Our home is with God, and we could not find Him by ourselves because of our disobedience. So God had to come to us. And where were we? Lost in pain, suffering, misery and ultimately death. Yes, that's right. We could easily miss this fact, so I'll say it again. We were lost in pain, suffering, misery and ultimately death. You see, if it were not for God, in the person of Jesus Christ, coming to meet us and "spend the night" with us in our suffering and death, we would never have been able to make it home in the morning. This world is like that night of darkness in the forest. Alone we are fearful, terrified and lost. But once Jesus finds us and we call out to Him, we realize that He has decided to join us on the very journey we are on—the journey of suffering and death as a result of sin. By entering into these consequences of sin with and for us, He is then able to take us by the hand "in the morning" and lead us back home. The morning being our final resurrection with Christ at the end of time.

The key to understanding this is that we were lost by disobedience. But God the Son was sent on a mission of obedient love, and He embraced it perfectly. He had to enter the "forest" of suffering and death to find us. He had to enter into the sleep of death with us. This was done out of love and as a perfect "yes" to the will of the Father. If we only cling to Him in His sleep of death, we will also rise with Him. But what we should focus on here is the choice of God to come to us. Sure, He could have left us on our own, lost and frightened. He could have left us abandoned. But He didn't. He chose to take on the consequences of our disobedience and suffer them Himself. It was His perfect way of reuniting us with Himself. It is an act of the greatest love and generosity. And He did not hesitate to experience it in every way.

A More Philosophical Explanation

For the more philosophical mind, let's look at it this way. Human nature is in a fallen state. It is a state of being that is contrary to the original intention of God. As explained in Chapter 2, we were made to live in this natural paradise with God. This is the state of Original Innocence. As a result of the disobedience of our first parents, all of humanity lost this state of innocence and now suffers the consequences. What are those consequences? Suffering and ultimately death. This is not God's fault. It is simply the natural effect of doing it our own way. But, again, God did not give up on us. God decided to take on our own human nature and enter into all the effects of our sin. He chose to unite divinity with fallen humanity by becoming one of us and entering into all that we suffer.

So the first key to understanding this is to understand the incredible effect of the Incarnation. We have to realize that because God took on our human nature and united that human nature to His divine nature, we begin our reunion with Him. But the reunion is not complete unless God, in His human nature, also experiences everything we do in our fallen state. And that includes death. He is now like us in all things except sin. But the good news comes later when we look at the Resurrection. This is the Good News because, if we let Him cling to us in our suffering and death, we can then, in turn, cling to Him in His Resurrection. More on this later, but for now the point at hand is that God's act of suffering and dying was an act of pure love to reunite us to God. Could He have done it another way? Perhaps. But He didn't. This is what He did; and when we understand what He did, we should be filled with nothing but incredible gratitude.

The New and Perfect Sacrifice

From the beginning of time, starting even with the children of Adam and Eve, we see what we call "prefigurements" of the one sacrifice of Christ. These are sin offerings. Offerings of one's labors such as food. But especially offerings of animals to God as sacrificial gifts. This practice is seen especially in the Temple when the priests would offer the sacrifices of lambs to God to atone for sin. Now, truth be told, none of these animal sacrifices could actually atone for sin. But they had a purpose. They were to prepare us for the one "Lamb" who would become a perfect sacrifice for all sin. Jesus is the one prefigured in all of these animal sacrifices. And He is the only sacrifice that truly takes away sin.

We are familiar with the phrase "The Lamb of God." As this "Lamb," Jesus spills His blood for the forgiveness of all sin. Furthermore, He is the one who freely sacrifices His life, so He is also the one Priest who does the offering. And the Cross becomes His altar of sacrifice. Though there is much that could be said about this from the point of view of biblical teaching, it is sufficient for our purposes to simply understand the concept of Jesus as the "Lamb of God who takes away the sins of the world."

Jesus is Buried

Jesus truly died. This means that His body and soul were separated. But there is something fascinating about His death that is unlike ours. It has to do with His burial.

Remember that Jesus' body was not anointed with the various oils and ointments. It was too late for this upon His death since the Passover was beginning. So Mark's Gospel tells us: "When the Sabbath was over, Mary Magdalene, Mary, the mother of James, and Salome bought spices so that they might go and anoint him" (Mk 16:1). But He was not there! He had risen!

Why is it significant that Jesus' body was never anointed? Because His body never needed to be anointed. In God's providence, this act of anointing the body was never done because Jesus' body never began to experience decay. This is one of the unique aspects of Jesus' body shared only with His mother. You see, the corruption of the body is a consequence of the fallen state of sin we are in. It's important to understand, though, that the corruption of the body is not part of the original plan and design of God for our bodies. And even though Jesus suffered and died, His body was still without sin and, thus, never experienced any of the consequences of sin. Therefore, when His body and soul separated, His body never fell into corruption.

The same is true for our Blessed Mother. As explained in Chapter 3, she was the Immaculate Conception, meaning she was preserved from all sin and never chose to sin. Therefore, she also was free from the corruption of the body. For that reason, we have always professed that, upon the completion of her life on Earth, she was taken body and soul into Heaven.

He Descended into Where?

In the Apostles' Creed, we say that Christ "descended into Hell." So what does that mean? How could Jesus go to Hell? Hell is a place of eternal separation from God; therefore, it seems strange to say Jesus went there, doesn't it?

This is the great mystery of Holy Saturday. On that day we ponder the silence of the tomb. But we also ponder another great mystery. We ponder the fact that Jesus' final leg of the mission He was sent to accomplish was accomplished only as His body lay in the tomb.

You see, at that time "Hell" was simply the "place," so to speak, where all those who had already died were present. It was the place of Abraham, Moses, the great prophets and also the great sinners. It was the abode of the dead. And it was called "Hell" only in that God was not present. He was not present, because Jesus had not reconciled humanity yet. So His descent to this abode of the dead was His way of bringing the Gospel to them. It was His final mission. And as the righteous in this place encountered Jesus, they were able to follow Him to the land of the Living in His Resurrection.

Once this act was accomplished, "Hell" took on a new form. Hell is now the place where only the damned are left, those who have freely rejected God and who live eternally separated from Him. So it may make more sense to us to say He "descended into the dead." But it's certainly proper to use the word "Hell" as long as we understand the difference between this temporary place of separation from God and the permanent one.

5

Death Has No Victory!

The Resurrection of Jesus is the crowning truth of our faith in Christ, a faith believed and lived as the central truth by the first Christian community; handed on as fundamental by Tradition; established by the documents of the New Testament; and preached as an essential part of the Paschal mystery along with the cross. (*CCC* #638)

Without the Resurrection of Jesus, all hope is lost, and there is no meaning to His death. The Resurrection makes it possible for us to share in His new life and is then followed by Jesus ascending into Heaven and sending the Holy Spirit. Let's look at some of the essential truths of the Resurrection so as to understand what it's all about.

A Real Historical Event

There was a specific day and time that Jesus rose from the dead. It happened in history and was witnessed by many. Mary Magdalene and the other Marys were the first to see Him. Soon after this, some of the Apostles saw Him. Some doubted, such as Thomas. Others saw and immediately believed. The process of coming to believe in the Resurrection of Jesus was a process dependent upon faith. Faith does come from seeing and hearing. It comes from hearing accounts of Jesus being alive and, for some, actually seeing it. Ultimately, the act of believing in the Resurrection required the inspired gift of faith. And this gift of faith produced knowledge of its truth. In other words, upon hearing or seeing, the person must be open to the gift of the Holy Spirit speaking in their soul, revealing the truth of Jesus' resurrection. So even though the Resurrection was a real and historical event, it was only properly understood and believed in by a gift of God speaking to one's soul.

Resurrection or Brought Back to Life?

Jesus did many miracles in His earthly life, including the amazing act of bringing some people back to life after they had died. For example, He raised Jairus' daughter from the dead (Mk 5) and also brought Lazarus, His friend, back to life (Jn 11). What did Jesus do in these two cases, and how did it differ from His Resurrection?

In both these cases, a person had died. Jesus came to them after death, gave a command, and they returned to life. They were the same as they were prior to death, everyone recognized them, and they were able to resume their lives. This is different from what happened with Jesus in His Resurrection. Jesus did not just come back to life. He did not just resume the life He had been living. No, Jesus was resurrected. He took on a new form of living. He now had a transformed and resurrected body. It was His old body that was resurrected, but it was different. With this new resurrected body, Jesus brought about a new potential existence for all humanity. This new body was physical but could also appear and disappear as was reported. Many who knew Him did not immediately recognize Him in this new resurrected state. He was different. He could eat but also suddenly appear behind closed doors. He carried the wounds of the crucifixion but was not wounded. He spoke and people listened with hearts set aflame.

It's important to understand this essential point of the Resurrection. Jesus takes on a new sort of physical existence. It's an existence that is now meant for all to share in, one day when the time comes for the final Judgment and the resurrection of all the dead. All of our bodies will be raised up, and those who are just will share in this new form of living. What is this new state? It's the glorified state. It's life with a new glorified body. Jesus still has this glorified body in Heaven, and it is this body that stands before the Father. So Jesus was not just raised up to His former state, He was transformed to the new physical existence we are all predestined to share in!

A Work of the Trinity

Jesus had the power to resurrect Himself, but it was not only His action. This was an action of the entire Trinity. It was the will of the Father and done by the power of the Holy Spirit. But, as in all of their works, the entire Trinity acted as one. They were united in their one divine will for a divine purpose.

It's also significant to point out that the Resurrection unites humanity itself to the Trinity in a new way. It brings this new resurrected and glorified human state into the life of God. The new resurrected and glorified human nature is now fully united to Christ, and He is united to the Father and the Spirit, which reveals the unity of humanity with the entire Trinity.

This points to the end and goal of all humanity. We now have hope for our own lives to share in this new glorified state of the Resurrection and union with the Trinity. We look forward to this and hope in this. And hope is not just something we wish for. True Christian hope is a virtue that is grounded in some divine truth revealed to us. We have true faith in the Resurrection, and this gift of faith also produces hope of achieving what we hope for. It's a hope and desire that is fully able to be realized, because this hope is instilled in us by God and by the reality of the Resurrection.

The Resurrection of Christ tells us that all humanity is now predestined by God's plan and by this historical act of the Resurrection to share in a new glorious state of life that goes even beyond the original intention of God in the Garden of Eden. We are now called to share in God's very life, united with Him in a new and glorious existence. This should fill us with excitement, wonder and awe!

The Veil is Lifted—The Ascension

Even after Jesus rose from the dead in His newly resurrected and glorified body, things were not complete. The *Catechism* states it this way:

> The veiled character of the glory of the Risen One during this time is intimated in his mysterious words to Mary Magdalene: "I have not yet ascended to the Father; but go to my brethren and say to them, I am ascending to my Father and your Father, to my God and your God" (Jn 20:17) This indicates a difference in manifestation between the glory of the risen Christ and that of the Christ exalted to the Father's right hand, a transition marked by the historical and transcendent event of the Ascension. (*CCC #660*)

What this means is that Jesus' glory, the glory of His resurrected and glorified state, cannot be seen in its fullness by human eyes until we also enter into the glories of Heaven. So Jesus appeared to the various disciples in a veiled way. His full glory was hidden from them.

Think back to the scene of the Transfiguration (Mt 17). This also was a revelation of this reality. For the moment, Jesus lifted but a part of the veil of His glory, and the Apostles were so overwhelmed that they fell face down. Now imagine this same Jesus, enjoying an even more glorified human state, with veil fully lifted in Heaven! It's beyond imagination. So for now, the best thing we can do is to realize that we cannot realize the glory of Christ's glorified state in Heaven.

But that is what He enjoys right now. Forty days after the Resurrection, Jesus ascended into Heaven to take His place at the right hand of the Father for all eternity. It was only there that the full veil of His glory was lifted eternally. So when we profess faith in His Resurrection and Ascension, we profess faith in this particular aspect also. And it should give us great hope and anticipation of encountering Him there.

We also should note that Jesus ascended by His own power. This is different than what we profess about Mary, His mother. We say she was "assumed" into Heaven body and soul. The difference is that Mary was taken to Heaven by the power of God. Jesus, being God, ascended on His own authority and by His own power. Of course, as with every other act of Christ, this was done in full union with the Father and the Holy Spirit. They acted as one, but they also acted individually. Each freely choosing and acting but acting in union making them one. Yes, this is hard to understand, but we need only to try and grasp the reality as best we can. It will be fully understood in Heaven.

At the Father's Right Hand

As Jesus ascended, He had to go somewhere. He ascended to some "place" since He was now in the form of a human and glorified body. This idea of a "place" is hard to understand and quite mysterious. Where is Heaven? Where is its physical location? Is it beyond the Universe? Is it in the Universe? The simple answer is that we do not really know. Many theologians have speculated about this, but I will not try to arrive at an answer. It is sufficient to simply raise the question and let that question sit as a mystery still to be understood.

But we can also say that this "place" Jesus ascended to is the right hand of the Father. The Father is not physical, but that's where Jesus is, body and soul. To be at the right hand of the Father especially points to the fact that Jesus is the Messiah and King. He sits on that "throne" to rule all of creation. And He will rule from that place for eternity. Again, the key here is to understand that the image of being at the Father's right hand is an image especially given to reveal to us Jesus' unique kingly authority now and for eternity.

His Return in Glory...and Grace

We say it every Sunday, "He will come again to judge the living and the dead..." But what does that mean? How and when will He return? To properly understand this, we must look at the three comings of Christ.

The first coming is all we have spoken of up until now. It's His Incarnation. He came at one specific moment in time, was born, lived, died and rose again. This coming was complete when He ascended.

There is a second coming we speak about constantly but do not always refer to it as a "coming." It's where we are right now in the history of salvation. It's Jesus coming to us daily by grace. It's His presence in the Sacraments. It's His abiding presence in the Church. It's His communication to us and His help given us through our life of prayer. And this is a real coming!

The section of the *Catechism* on the Sacraments and Prayer reveals the full scope of this coming by grace. So for now, it's just worth mentioning and identifying as a real coming of Christ. This is important because when Jesus ascended into Heaven, He did not abandon us. He did not leave and tell us He'd be back, that we should be good while He's gone and that He's looking forward to meeting us again one day. No, He said He would be with us always until the end of time. That means He'd be with us until that final coming which we will speak of next. But this coming by grace is essential for us to understand.

Once He took His seat at the right hand of the Father, He sent the Holy Spirit and the Church began. The Church will also be covered in Chapter 7, but it's important to mention now that the Church is a true coming of Christ here and now. It's Jesus, the King and Messiah, who is governing us and directing our lives in an active way through our life of prayer, the Sacraments, and the hierarchy. It's Jesus who speaks to us through the Saints, the Scriptures, and one another. He is alive and active in our world here and now, and He is establishing His Kingdom here and now. More on this later. For now let's look at His final and glorious coming.

A Time of Judgment

The third and final coming is when Jesus returns to Earth in splendor and glory. It will be "the end of the world as we know it." It will be a time when His permanent Kingdom is established. There is much to say about this moment in history, and it is actually quite fascinating to reflect upon. Before you read on, open the *Catechism of the Catholic Church* and read paragraphs #671–677.

Wow! That's good stuff! It almost reads as a deeply intriguing futuristic science fiction mystery novel. The only difference is that it's all true, it's all glorious, and it's all beyond any mystery we will ever be able to comprehend until it actually takes place. And it will take place at one definitive moment in time to come!

So what does this all mean? It means that Jesus will be returning in all His splendor and glory. He will physically return to Earth one day, radiant and glorious. We will see Him, and the world as we currently know it will come to an end. At that moment in time, God will establish

His permanent Kingdom, and both Heaven and Earth will be united as one. It will be "a new Heaven and a new Earth" (Rv 21:1). The former Heaven and Earth will pass away and the new order will be established.

But that's not all! At that moment in time all the dead shall rise. That's right, all people who have ever died will rise. This means that everybody who has been "laid to rest" in a cemetery or elsewhere will be brought back to life, given a new glorified body, and that body will be rejoined to his or her soul.

The *Catechism* also states:

> When he comes at the end of time to judge the living and the dead, the glorious Christ will reveal the secret disposition of hearts and will render to each man according to his works and according to his acceptance or refusal of grace. (#682)

This is a fascinating thought—and a bit scary, too! It means that all that is hidden will come to light. This can be good or bad depending upon what is hidden. The thought should both fill us with a bit of holy fear, and it should also fill us with a holy joy. The holy fear is actually a gift from God to help us eliminate any secret and hidden sin we have now or have struggled with in the past. Since it will in fact all come to light one day, we might as well deal with it now so that our sin is no more. If we do, even our sin is turned into virtue and grace. And then, at the end of time, that grace and virtue is what will be made manifest. This manifestation of our virtue will be the cause of holy joy not only for us but also for others to whom it is manifested.

We will be judged, then, based on what is there within our conscience. It will no longer just be exterior. We will not be able to put on a good face and pretend we are someone we are not. The full truth will come out and will be made manifest for all to see in accord with God's plan.

Another thing to note is that at the Final Judgment even those who are in Hell will rise. Why? Because as humans we are meant to eternally be united with our bodies. We are, in essence, body and soul. So even the dead will receive their bodies back. But sadly, they will then suffer eternally not only spiritually but also physically. What this actually entails we do not know. But it will be a real pain of loss. Loss of God and loss in that the body and soul will not be able to share in life with God. This can seem harsh and unfair, but we should remind ourselves that God is perfectly just and perfectly loving and however this eternal loss and eternal suffering is lived, it is right and just.

What will this new life look like for those who share in the resurrection to new life? It will be life with God, physically and spiritually, as well as life with each other. The Book of Revelation speaks symbolically of this new life as a city where God is on the throne in the center of the city. Light shines forth from Him, so there is no need for the sun or moon. The streets are gold. The gates filled with precious stones. And so much more. This symbolic language should not be taken literally; rather, it should be seen as imagery that helps us understand the beauty, splendor, and magnificence of the life that awaits us. It's the new Heavens and new Earth. I can't wait!

Will Cremated Bodies Also Rise?

One interesting note on this is our customs in cemeteries. First, as I mentioned, we say the person is "laid to rest." This language comes from the belief that death is temporary. Each body is in the "sleep of death" and awaiting that final resurrection. In Catholic cemeteries, we even have the custom of burying a person facing the East. The reason for this is that the "East" is said to be from where Jesus will return. Perhaps it's just symbolism. We really have no way of knowing, literally, how this Second Coming will take place. But as an act of faith, we acknowledge this return from the East by burying our loved ones in a position so that when they do rise, they will be facing the East.

Some may be curious about those who have been cremated or who died in a fire or in some other way that involved a destruction of the body. That's easy. If God can make the Universe out of nothing, then He certainly can bring together any earthly remains no matter where or what form these remains are in. But it does bring up a good point to address regarding cremation.

Today, cremation is becoming more and more common. The Church does permit cremation but adds some specific guidelines for cremation.

The purpose of the guidelines is to safeguard our faith in the resurrection of the body. The bottom line is that as long as the intention of cremation in no way conflicts with faith in the resurrection of the body, then cremation is permitted. In other words, what we do with our earthly remains after death, or with those of our loved ones, reveals what we believe. So what we do should reflect clearly our beliefs. Let me give an example to illustrate. If someone were to be cremated and wanted to have their ashes sprinkled in Wrigley Field because they were a die-hard Cubs fan and wanted to always be with the Cubs, this would be a problem of faith. Why? Because having ashes sprinkled that way does not make a person one with the Cubs. Furthermore, by doing something like this it ignores the fact that they are to be laid to rest with the hope and belief in their future resurrection.

But there are some practical reasons for cremation that make it acceptable at times. It can be less expensive and, therefore, necessary for some families to consider given the high costs of a funeral, it may allow for couples to be buried together in the same grave, it may allow the family to more easily transport their loved one's remains to another part of the country where the final burial will take place (such as in their town of birth). In these instances the reason for cremation is more practical than having anything to do with faith.

One last key point to mention is that cremated remains should be buried. This is part of the whole Catholic ritual and mirrors Jesus' own death, burial and resurrection. So burial is also a matter of faith.

6

The Holy Spirit

What is the Holy Spirit?

What is the Holy Spirit? Good question. It's easy to think of the Holy Spirit as a powerful force from God. Or a mysterious aspect of God's life. It's confusing to many. So what is the Holy Spirit? The proper question is not "what" but "Who." "Who is the Holy Spirit" is the right question because the Holy Spirit is a Person. A divine Person. Equal in dignity and majesty with the Father and the Son. The Holy Spirit is one member of the Holy Trinity. As a Person, the Holy Spirit is one we can be in relation with. We can know and love the Holy Spirit just as we know and love the Father and the Son. And the Spirit loves us just as He loves the Father and the Son. Personhood means there is potential for love and union. The Holy Spirit has an intellect and will and with those characteristics freely knows and loves as God.

At the beginning of time, we were slowly made aware of the reality of God the Father. The Great I AM. It was revealed to us through the prophets and patriarchs that there was one God and only one. But as time passed, we were also made aware of the Messiah who was the Son of God. As we came to know this Son, in the person of Jesus, we came to realize that He also was I AM. He also was God. Then the Son began to reveal to us that He would send His Advocate, the Holy Spirit. And we came to realize that this Holy Spirit is also God, also I AM. Confused? We shouldn't be. This was God's way of slowly revealing the full truth of Who He is over time. He is One, yet He is also Three. One God, three divine Persons.

We say, in philosophical language, that the Holy Spirit is "consubstantial" with the Father and the Son, and with the Father and the Son is adored and glorified. To be "consubstantial" means that God the Holy Spirit is of the same divine substance or the same divine nature as the Father and the Son. "Con" means "with," and "substantial" means "substance." Again, this is philosophical terminology that our Church has used to try to vaguely put into language the relationships between these three divine Persons. And they are the only three Persons who share in this one divine nature. It also means that they act in perfect unity. They share the same will and act in unison in fulfilling this will. They share the same power as God and act as one God.

Being of the same substance means that each Person of the Trinity shares in all the same qualities of this nature. And what are these divine qualities that they each share in? They have all-power, are all-knowing, and are all-loving. They are perfection! And this perfect sharing in these attributes unites them and enables them to act as one.

We also learn that the Holy Spirit has spoken to us already through the prophets. This means that the Holy Spirit did not just appear after Jesus ascended into Heaven. The Holy Spirit did not just start to act at that time. Rather, the Holy Spirit has been active with the Father and the Son from all eternity. It's just that we only came to a fuller understanding of this Person of the Trinity after Jesus' ascension. The works of the Holy Spirit were revealed to us more fully after this time, helping us to understand Him as a divine Person.

But it's also important to point out that the age we are in now, the age after the life, death, resurrection and ascension of the Son, is especially the age of the Holy Spirit! This is the time when the Holy Spirit is especially active in our world and in the Church. The Father is especially seen and revealed in the creation of the world, the Son is especially seen and revealed in the redemption of the world after it fell from innocence, and the Holy Spirit is now clearly seen and revealed as the one active in our lives and in the Church sanctifying (making holy) all who follow Jesus and all who seek the will of the Father.

It is the Holy Spirit who is given to us in baptism. At that time, we are made adopted children of the Father, we are made one in Jesus the Son, and we are filled with the Holy Spirit to live out our new Christian calling as sons and daughters of God in Christ Jesus. Now that's saying a lot. So let's take a closer look at the activity of the Holy Spirit.

Where Do We Meet the Holy Spirit?

It is the role of the Holy Spirit to enkindle within us the grace we need in order to know Jesus Christ as our Lord and Savior and to know the Father as our Father. The Holy Spirit makes us who we are as Christians.

The Holy Spirit also has the unique role of animating the Church in our day and age. The "Church" here means everyone who is alive in Christ. Everyone who has grace in their lives. Everyone following the will of the Father and living out their Christian dignity as sons and daughters of God. The Holy Spirit makes this happen in a perfect and orchestrated way.

As we look at the workings of the Holy Spirit, we see various ways that He has and continues to work in our lives and in the life of the Church. The *Catechism* #688, spells those ways out like this. We know the Holy Spirit...

—in the Scriptures he inspired;

—in the Tradition, to which the Church Fathers are always timely witnesses;

—in the Church's Magisterium, which he assists;

—in the sacramental liturgy, through its words and symbols, in which the Holy Spirit puts us into communion with Christ;

—in prayer, wherein he intercedes for us;

—in the charisms and ministries by which the Church is built up;

—in the signs of apostolic and missionary life;

—in the witness of saints through whom he manifests his holiness and continues the work of salvation.

Let's take a look at each one of these so as to gain a better understanding of the workings of the Holy Spirit.

—in the Scriptures he inspired;

The human author of each book of the Scriptures, as explained in Chapter 1, is a true author of the Holy Scriptures. Through that person, each particular book of the Scriptures was written. The human author's unique personality and experiences shine through. But the human author is not the only one writing the book or letter. We also profess that the human author wrote under the guidance and inspiration of the Holy Spirit! It was the Spirit who guided each word revealing what He wanted written. It was a joint effort and 100% of both their works. This shows the power of the Holy Spirit to act in us and to use us as instruments. Yes, He acted in a very unique and powerful way when He inspired the human authors of the Scriptures in their writings. This is not something the Holy Spirit will do again, inspiring more Scripture to be written. But the fact that the human author was inspired and was used as such a powerful instrument should tell us not only much about this wonderful gift of the Bible, it should also tell us much about the fact that the Holy Spirit wants to use us humans for divine work. He wants to inspire each and every one of us for a powerful work He has given only to us. Not in the same way that He once inspired the books of the Bible, but certainly in powerful ways nonetheless. When this is properly understood, we should be in awe and greatly anticipate what God has in mind for us while we travel this pilgrimage on earth!

—in the Tradition, to which the Church Fathers are always timely witnesses;

—in the Church's Magisterium, which he assists;

Jesus established the Church and bestowed the Spirit upon the Apostles who were His first bishops with Peter being the first pope. This bestowing of the Holy Spirit is seen in John 20:22. In that verse, the resurrected Jesus is appearing to the Apostles in the upper room behind closed doors. After appearing to them, the Scripture says that "He breathed on them and said to them 'receive the Holy Spirit...'" It was especially with this act that these Apostles were given what they needed to begin their ministry and, in part, to begin to establish what we refer to as "Sacred Tradition." We will say more about this later, but for now suffice it to say that "Sacred Tradition" is not just the establishment of various cultural or human traditions. When we speak of "traditions" with a small "t", we are only speaking of human customs and practices that are established throughout time. But when we speak of "Tradition" with a capital "T," we speak of the work of the Holy Spirit to continue teaching and guiding us through the successors of the Apostles in every day and age. Tradition is the word used to specify the teaching action of the Holy Spirit in every age. And this is important! Why? Because Jesus did not give us a 500 volume book of the law addressing each and every question that would ever arise in the areas of faith and morality. No, instead He gave us the Holy Spirit, and most specifically, He gave the unique gift of the Holy Spirit to the Apostles and their successors to teach us and to lead us into all truth in every day and age when questions would arise. This is Tradition, and it is quite an ongoing gift!

—in the sacramental liturgy, through its words and symbols, in which the Holy Spirit puts us into communion with Christ;

The Sacramental Liturgy is the most powerful way that God is present to us right here, right now. The Liturgy is a work of the Holy Spirit where the entire Trinity is made present. In the Liturgy, we use words and symbols through which God shows up and is made manifest. We do not see Him with our eyes, but He is there. He is there in His fullness, veiled by the liturgical action itself. Much more will be said on this later on in Book Two of this series: *My Catholic Worship!* But for now this brief introduction will suffice.

Among the greatest of these actions is the Most Holy Eucharist. In the Eucharist, we have a unity of Heaven and Earth. God comes to meet us, to descend to us, and we encounter Him. This is done by an action of the Holy Spirit alive within the Church. You can say that it's a joint action of the Church and the Holy Spirit, and this mutual activity brings forth the very real presence of Christ our Lord.

By "joint action" I mean that the Church, in the person of the priest, speaks and acts using the assigned words, matter and actions (i.e., extending hands over bread and wine while speaking the words of consecration). It is this action that also guarantees the working of the Holy Spirit to make present the Savior of the world in a real and sacramental way.

God is also made present to us in all liturgical actions, but above all, it is the Holy Eucharist that we hold up as the summit of His presence!

—in prayer, wherein he intercedes for us;

We do not even know how to pray by ourselves. Turning to God, surrendering to Him, seeking Him and listening to Him all requires an action of the Holy Spirit upon us. That's right, we need God's help to pray to God. It's an interesting reality.

Why is this the case? Because true prayer is something that must be a response to God. What I mean is that we can "say prayers" if we like, and this is good. We can initiate "prayers." But there is a difference between "true prayer" and "prayers that are said." True prayer is when God, by an action of the Holy Spirit, speaks to us and draws us by an interior calling. God the Holy Spirit takes the initiative by way of an invitation. And we, on our part, respond. We respond to God calling and speaking, and this begins a process of prayer. Prayer is communication with God, and the ultimate form of communication we are called to have with God in prayer is surrender and love. It is in this high form of prayer that we discover God acting in our lives and transforming us. And this is an action of the Holy Spirit. The Holy Spirit "intercedes for us" insofar as the Holy Spirit acts on us, transforming us into a member of Christ Himself, so as to present us to the Father in Heaven. The intercession is our transformation in Christ.

—in the charisms and ministries by which the Church is built up;
—in the signs of apostolic and missionary life;
—in the witness of saints through whom he manifests his holiness and continues the work of salvation.

The Holy Spirit is also very much alive in the activity of the Church. It is the Holy Spirit who gives charisms. A charism is a spiritual gift given to someone for the good of the Church. It's a sort of spiritual quality or ability to offer some service to the Church. Charisms could be as amazing as being prophetic or healing the sick, or they could be as ordinary (but necessary) as being able to organize activities within the Church in an exemplary way. The key to a charism is that it is for the good of the Church and the spreading of the Gospel.

Charisms are especially necessary for the apostolic and missionary activity of the Church. As members of the Church, we are called to evangelize by spreading the Gospel far and wide. To do this effectively, and in accord with God's plan, we need His grace and action in our lives. We need special charism (gifts) to accomplish this responsibility. It is the task of the Holy Spirit to bestow these gifts.

The saints are the great witnesses of God. God's light and goodness shine on them and through them for all to see. It is especially the Holy Spirit who enables these great saints to be shining examples of God's love for all to see.

Images of the Holy Spirit

There are many ways the Holy Spirit has been revealed to us throughout the ages. There have been many images of the Holy Spirit used in Scripture. Each one of these images reveals a unique characteristic of the Holy Spirit. Here are some of those images:

Breath: The best translation for the term "Spirit" is "Ruah" or breath, air or wind. The Holy Spirit is the "Holy Breath of God." This image is seen in various places in the Scriptures. For example, John 20:22 says that Jesus "breathed on them and said to them, 'receive the Holy Spirit.'" The breath of God or wind of God is seen many places in the Scriptures, as we will see in our next section.

Water: Water signifies the Holy Spirit in that it is poured and cleanses. It is poured at baptism, and the Holy Spirit is subsequently poured in that act. Water also signifies death to sin. This is seen in the story of Noah and the flood as well as in the story of the Red Sea when water destroyed the Egyptian army.

Anointing: The symbol of anointing with oil also signifies an outpouring of the Holy Spirit. We see this in several of the sacraments (Baptism, Confirmation, Anointing of the Sick, and Holy Orders). Also, the prophets were anointed with oil to symbolize the outpouring of the Holy Spirit on them for their ministry.

Fire: Fire transforms that which it touches. It symbolizes power, energy and transformation. It was "tongues as of fire" that descended upon the Apostles at Pentecost.

Cloud and light: We see these images in the Old and New Testament. Jesus was transfigured in light. Mary was overshadowed by the Holy Spirit. It was a pillar of cloud by day and a pillar of fire by night that led the Israelites through the desert. The cloud is a masking and veiling of the presence of the Spirit, and the light is but a small portion of the radiance of the Holy Spirit shining forth.

Seal: To be marked or sealed with God is an action of the Holy Spirit. We say, for example, in Confirmation that there is an indelible character, a spiritual character, a seal, that is impressed upon one's soul. This is a marking of God and a sign of the presence of the Holy Spirit.

Hand: The laying on of hands is a sign of the outpouring of the Holy Spirit. This is seen in Baptism, Confirmation, Ordination and the Anointing of the Sick. We also recall that Jesus laid hands on the sick to cure them.

Finger: It was by the "finger" of God that Jesus did many great works. This shows the Holy Spirit at work in Jesus' ministry. It was the finger of God that gave the Ten Commandments. And it is by the finger of God that the Holy Spirit continues to work in our day and age.

Dove: Perhaps this is the most common symbol of the Holy Spirit. The dove was present with Noah at the ark, the dove descended upon Jesus at His baptism. White is a symbol of purity, and its wings give it swiftness and agility to descend from the Heavens.

The Holy Spirit's Activity in Salvation History

The Holy Spirit has been around from before the beginning of time and has been made manifest throughout the history of our Universe. Let's look at the various ways the Holy Spirit has been at work:

Creation: The Spirit breathed on the waters at the beginning of Creation and is responsible for the principle of life. If you think hard about it, you'll discover that "life" is hard to define. What actually gives life? What sustains life? Be it plants, animals or humans, no scientific discovery can unmask the actual principle of life itself. Much can be said about living creatures and how they work from a scientific perspective. But *why* they work is another question. And the answer is the Holy Spirit who animates and sustains all life.

Promise, Theophanies, and the Law: God spoke to Moses, Joshua and the great prophets in various ways. These manifestations of God's presence are theophanies. The law, given through Moses, was also a manifestation of God's order and direction. All of these point to the promise of God's future gift of salvation. A theophany is a manifestation of God, by the working of the Holy Spirit, pointing to the promise of God that will ultimately be fulfilled by the Holy Spirit.

Kingdom: The kingdoms of the Old Testament also pointed to the promise of the one eternal Kingdom which would be established by Christ and orchestrated by the Holy Spirit. These O.T. kingdoms would fall as people failed to live by the law which was revealed by the Spirit. Thus, their inability to keep the law was a sign they needed more. They needed the fullness of the outpouring of the Holy Spirit. This pointed over and over again to the need for a Messiah. That Messiah would come and, in the end, bestow the Holy Spirit.

John the Baptist: John was "filled with the Holy Spirit" from his mother's womb. He was the greatest of the prophets who spoke with the anointing of the Spirit of God. It is by John's hand that Jesus was baptized after which the Holy Spirit descended in manifest form.

Our Blessed Mother: The Holy Spirit prepared Mary with a special preservative grace (as explained in Chapter 3). This grace was given by a special working of the Holy Spirit by applying the merits of her Son's death and Resurrection to her at the moment of her conception. She then lived her early life filled with the Holy Spirit. At the Annunciation, Mary conceived her Savior, and the Savior of the whole world, "by the power of the Holy Spirit."

Jesus: Jesus is the "Anointed One." He is filled with the Holy Spirit and one with the Holy Spirit. At His baptism, the Spirit descends in fullness upon Him. Not that the Holy Spirit wasn't already with Him fully. Rather, this was a manifestation of the Spirit who was already with Jesus revealing this reality. Jesus promised His Advocate, the Holy Spirit, to His disciples. In the end, at His death He "gave up His Spirit." And after His Resurrection He breathed the Spirit on the Apostles and promised to send His Spirit on all as He was preparing to ascend into Heaven.

Pentecost: Pentecost is the clearest manifestation of the Holy Spirit. As the disciples are gathered in the upper room, tongues as of fire descend upon them, and they are filled with the Holy Spirit. They receive various charisms and are given a new strength and boldness to proclaim the Gospel.

Church: At Pentecost the Church is born. We see the Holy Spirit alive in various ways in the Church today. As outlined earlier in this Chapter, the Holy Spirit is the one teaching through the bishops, sanctifying us through prayer and the sacraments, and spreading the Good News through the apostolic works of the Church.

So the Holy Spirit has been very much alive and active in the history of our world and continues to be active in the life of the Church. This brings us to the next chapter on the Church itself!

7

The Church:
The Living Body of Christ

"The Church" is the People that God gathers in the whole world. She exists in local communities and is made real as a liturgical, above all a Eucharistic, assembly. She draws her life from the word and the Body of Christ and so herself becomes Christ's Body (*CCC* #752).

Is Jesus really gone from us? Is His body truly ascended? Yes and no. Yes, He has ascended to the right hand of the Father. But no, He's not gone. He is very much alive today in the Church. The Church **is** His body, and it is a living presence of Christ. This takes a bit of prayerful reflection to understand.

When Jesus Ascended, He promised to send the Advocate, the Holy Spirit. When the Holy Spirit descended, the Church was born. And as the Holy Spirit continues to descend, the Church carries on. We, as members of the Church, become de facto members of the Body of Christ. We are His hands and feet, His mouth and heart. We become Christ's living presence. This is important to understand properly. First, we should not think that somehow "I am Christ" because of my own good deeds. No, what we mean is that Christ has chosen to live in us insofar as we let Him in. And as we let Him in, it is He who lives in us! To be a member of Christ Jesus is first and foremost His action in our lives. This should leave us with gratitude, humility and awe.

Some Initial Distinctions

Before we get started with an understanding of the Church, we need to make some initial distinctions. We have to make a distinction between

"Catholic" (with a capital C) and "catholic" (with a small c). We also should make a distinction between the "Catholic Church" and the "Church of Christ." Bear with me on this. It may seem confusing at first, but it's worth the effort. Here are the distinctions:

Church of Christ: This is the broadest definition of the Church. It refers to the Church as God sees it in its fullness. It refers to each and every person on Earth, in Purgatory and in Heaven who are united to Christ. It refers to everyone united to Christ individually as well as all organized groups of people (churches and Christian communities) who are, even in a minimal way, united to Christ and either on the road to salvation or are already there. It could even include individuals who, through no fault of their own, do not know Christ explicitly yet follow His voice in their conscience. So this is the big picture. It's the full picture of the Church, and this is what we are speaking of throughout in all the symbols and images of the Church.

Catholic Church: This is Catholic with a capital "C." By this we mean the Roman Catholic Church led by the pope in Rome. Within the Catholic Church, the fullness of the Church of Christ resides. In other words, it's all here! The teachings, the grace, the witness of faith, the missionary activity, etc. It's the most visible and full sign of the Church of Christ there is on Earth. This doesn't mean that other Christians can't be a member of the Body of Christ, because they can. But only the Catholic Church contains the full outpouring of grace and truth. The Catholic Church is, casually speaking, "the real deal!"

catholic: This is catholic with a small "c." This refers to one unique aspect of the Church of Christ—its universality! We will see this later in this chapter when we speak of the Four Marks of the Church.

Symbols of the Church

One way the Scriptures teach us about the many truths of our faith is through the use of symbolic images. This use of symbolic images applies to the Church also. Here are some images in Scripture that give us insight into the Church:

People of God: Shows we belong to God. He has a certain "ownership" of us. This also shows that the Church is chosen from the people who have rejected God and are not His people. This means that God's people are those who have responded to being called back to Him and out of the group of those who are lost. As the People of God, we are called to share in the threefold mission of Christ: Priest, Prophet and King. (1) Priest: We offer our lives as a sacrifice to the Father. (2) Prophet: We continue to spread the Gospel everywhere by words and deeds. (3) King: We govern our own souls, our families and all of society in accord with God's will.

Body of Christ: Christ is our Head and we are His body. We are members of His very life and person, but He is still our head. As members of His body, we are intimately united to Him. We are not just His followers, and He is not just our example, rather, we share in His life and He is our head.

Sheepfold: An enclosure for sheep. We are the **Flock**, and the Church is the full sheepfold. Christ is the Shepherd.

Cultivated Field: The Church is truly a rich land which bears an abundance of good fruit. It is truly rich soil.

Building of God: Christ is the cornerstone on which the Church is built and is the dwelling place of God and His people.

The Bride of Christ: We are wedded to Christ, united with Him as one.

Temple of the Holy Spirit: The human soul and body are inseparable. Their unity makes up the human person. In the same way, the Body of Christ and the Holy Spirit are intimately united just as soul and body. They are one and function as one. Thus, the Holy Spirit, dwelling in the Body of Christ, is the Church. One manifestation of the Holy Spirit in the Church is the many charisms alive in the Church. A charism is a special gift given to individual members of the Body of Christ to be used for the upbuilding of the Church. There are numerous charisms, such as good administration, prophetic teaching, extraordinary compassion for the poor, and much more. There are also some unique charisms, such as the gift of healing and other miraculous gifts.

Our Mother: We are born into new life through this new mother the Church. We also see our Blessed Mother in this role, which we will further examine later in the chapter. But for now, we see her as an image of the Church in that all who are born anew in grace are born anew from her in her Son Jesus. She is the Mother of the Son of God; therefore, she is the Mother of those who make up the members of the Body of her Son.

A Bit of Historical Perspective

Why did God create the Universe? Simple answer. It was for the Church. The Church was in the Father's mind from eternity and all He created was so that the Church would have a place to exist. The People of God, the Body of Christ, the Sheepfold, etc., all exist within this wonderful Universe God created. And it is for this Church that He created all things.

At the beginning of time, our first parents sinned and broke their relationship with God. Communion with Him was lost. But it was at that very moment that God the Father began preparing us to be gathered back to Himself in the Church, the Body of His Son. He wanted to look upon us and, once again, see His sons and daughters. This is the Church!

Slowly, over time, God began to prepare and gather a people unto Himself. He began to gather a people to Himself who would love Him freely and be reunited with Him in His Son by the working of the Holy Spirit. He did this as He made a covenant with Noah, and Abraham, and all the patriarchs and prophets afterwards. Little by little God began to establish a new order and a new relationship with the people He created. And little by little He began what would become the Church.

When the Son took on flesh and became one of us, the potential for union with God was put into full motion. His death then destroyed death itself, and His resurrection enabled all who share His human nature to also rise with Him. We die to sin and rise in grace. This action in our daily lives unites us to Christ, thus making us members of the Church.

Jesus establishes His Kingdom, and that Kingdom will come into full bloom in the future when He returns in all glory, destroying all sin and death for eternity. But His Kingdom and governance is already established in the Church today as we give our lives to Him and allow Him to govern us. In this act, we become members of this new Kingdom which is called the Church.

The Mystery of the Church

The Church is both physical and spiritual. It is human and divine. It is Christ and His people living together in unity as one. This is a great mystery. But it is also a glorious reality. Saint Bernard of Clairvaux puts it this way:

> O humility! O sublimity! Both tabernacle of cedar and sanctuary of God; earthly dwelling and celestial palace; house of clay and royal hall; body of death and temple of light; and at last both object of scorn to the proud and bride of Christ! She is black but beautiful, O daughters of Jerusalem, for even if the labor and pain of her long exile may have discolored her, yet heaven's beauty has adorned her (St. Bernard of Clairvaux, *In Cant. Sermo* 27:14: PL 183:920D). (*CCC* #771)

The Church is also seen as a sacrament of God. By "sacrament" we are not just speaking of the seven Sacraments. Rather, we see the Church as a "sacrament" by analogy. Perhaps, in a certain sense, we could call the Church the eighth sacrament, at least in an analogous way. A sacrament is a physical reality, a sign with actions and matter that brings about the true presence of Christ in the world. It's a way of uniting Heaven and Earth. Well, the Church is the same reality. Through the physical aspects of the Church, the divine aspects are transmitted. Through the pope and bishops, the Gospel is transmitted in every day and age in a definitive way. Through the sacraments, the life of grace is given. Through missionaries, the Gospel is spread to all peoples. And through the holiness of each and every member, God is made manifest!

So the Church as a sacrament means that Heaven comes to Earth in a real and powerful way. God dwells in His people, in the Liturgy, and in the hierarchy of the Church in various ways. It is this wedding of God with us that makes up His Church!

Marks of the Church

Traditionally, we speak of the "Four Marks of the Church" as being four unique and foundational qualities of the Church. These four marks speak to the essence of what the Church is and gives us insight into God, as well, as we ponder the way He designed the Church itself. The Four Marks are: One, Holy, Catholic and Apostolic.

One: All of us realize that there are countless religions and there are even countless Christian denominations. As we look at the history of Christianity, we can find that there were numerous conflicts that led to splits and to the founding of new churches. But there is no new *Church*, there are only new *churches*. What I mean is that there is only one Body of Christ, there is only one Church and that one Church is the Church of Christ Jesus. We believe and profess that this one Church of Christ is found, in its fullness, within the Catholic Church. As Vatican II is quoted in the *Catechism*:

> "For it is through Christ's Catholic Church alone, which is the universal help toward salvation, that the fullness of the means of salvation can be obtained. It was to the apostolic college alone, of which Peter is the head, that we believe that our Lord entrusted all the blessings of the New Covenant, in order to establish on earth the one Body of Christ into which all those should be fully incorporated who belong in any way to the People of God" (UR 3 § 5). (*CCC* #816)

So the key here is to be able to distinguish between "The Church" and "The Catholic Church." We say that the Catholic Church is the instrument through which the fullness of the Church and salvation is found. But the Church of Christ is also found outside of the visible structures of the Catholic Church to a lesser degree. Interestingly, though, we would still say that, in a sense, everyone who is a member of Christ is still, in a very real way, a member of His one Catholic Church...*they just don't know it!*

The key principle at work here is that of unity. Christ is one, and His body is one. This unity comes about especially through charity and faith. It comes about because we are united in love and faith with Christ our head. But with that said, there is also incredible diversity in the Church. Diversity is NOT disunity. Rather, diversity actually can help to foster true unity. Diversity refers to the various cultures, languages, traditions and expressions of faith. So, the concrete way that one worships in Africa may look very different from the way one worships in Europe, Indonesia, Mexico or the United States. The way we worship today may look different than the way Christians did 500 years ago. Though the expression may be different and diverse, the faith and charity are the same. And for that reason, diversity of cultural expression and the like actually help foster true unity on the deeper level of charity and faith. In other words, because we are diverse on the more superficial levels, our unity must take place on the deeper level. And that deeper level is faith and love. This is true unity!

It's kind of like the husband and wife, or two best friends, who share very little in regard to common interests. One likes sports, the other likes crafts. One likes to read, the other likes to go out. They will most likely not find unity in their ordinary interests. But this can be good. It can be good because it will force them to find unity on a deeper and far more important level. They will have to find unity on the level of their love and care for each other rather than just a love of common interests. So it is with the variety of expressions of our faith. This enables and invites the Church to be united in the essentials rather than the expressions.

Interestingly, even sin and division force those within the Church to unity. Sin, for example, forces us to seek mutual mercy and reconciliation. It enables us to forgive (an act of mercy) and to ask for forgiveness. So all things can potentially work toward the good and unity of the Church in Christ Jesus!

So whatever may initially seem to be a cause for disunity (cultural diversity, sin, disagreement, division), in the end forces us to seek unity on an even deeper level of grace, mercy and faith. This is essential, because if we want to be members of the Body of Christ, then we want to be united with every other member, also. And this desire and commitment will enable us to be open to Christ bringing about this unity within His one Church!

Holy: If the Church is the Bride of Christ, the Body of Christ, and the Temple of the Holy Spirit, then the Church is, by necessity, not only united as one but is also holy. It's not possible to be united to Christ so intimately and, at the same time, to lack holiness. In fact, the more we sin, the less a member of the Church we become. So if we are to become full living members of the Church, then we must individually become holy. We must become saints!

The heart of holiness is charity. Therefore, insofar as each one of us grows in charity, we also grow in holiness. Saint Thérèse of Lisieux is quoted in the *Catechism* in coming to this discovery:

> If the Church was a body composed of different members, it couldn't lack the noblest of all; *it must have a Heart, and a Heart BURNING WITH LOVE.* And I realized that *this love alone* was the true motive force which enabled the other members of the Church to act; if it ceased to function, the Apostles would forget to preach the gospel, the Martyrs would refuse to shed their blood. LOVE, IN FACT, IS THE VOCATION WHICH INCLUDES ALL OTHERS; IT'S A UNIVERSE OF ITS OWN, COMPRISING ALL TIME AND SPACE—IT'S ETERNAL! (*CCC* #826)

The story Saint Thérèse tells is a powerful one in her spiritual autobiography. She shares that she was desirous of fulfilling so many different missions within the Church. She longed to be a missionary, pondered what it would be like to be a priest, and continued to seek what her role was within the Church, within the Body of Christ. One day it hit her. She discovered her mission was to be the heart of Christ, the heart of the Church. And, in being the heart, she was to be love. And in being love, she was to be all things.

Now this is holiness! And it is this discovery of being love and living love that make the Church truly holy!

Our Blessed Mother is the supreme model of holiness in the Church because she is perfectly filled with love. Therefore, she is perfectly holy.

Catholic: The Church is also "catholic," meaning it is universal. Here we are speaking of catholic with a small "c." By "universal" we mean two things:

1) The Church is first of all complete. In the Church is the fullness of salvation because in the Church is Christ Jesus. So it is universal, full and complete because the Church is the Body of Christ.

2) The Church is also universal insofar as it is open to all people and is sent to bring all people into her fold. We have a mission to evangelize and to invite everyone into the fold of Christ. You do not have to be born into the Church, rather, you have to be reborn into Christ, and it is this act that is open to all.

So what about all those non-Catholics? Or what about the non-Christians? What about the Muslims, Jews, and even atheists? Is there any hope for them?

Let's start with the atheist. One of the Vatican II documents explains it this way:

> Those who, through no fault of their own, do not know the Gospel of Christ or his Church, but who nevertheless seek God with a sincere heart, and, moved by grace, try in their actions to do his will as they know it through the dictates of their conscience—those too may achieve eternal salvation (LG 16; cf. DS 3866–3872). (*CCC* #847)

Now with that said, it's also important to explain that this sort of person, a person who "through no fault of their own," fails to come to discover the explicit truths of God, namely, all that is revealed in Scripture and through the Magisterium, may actually still be saved. How? By following God in their conscience. This shows us that salvation is first and foremost something offered to us internally. And when someone has never been given the opportunity to discover salvation externally, God can still speak to them interiorly. If they listen, they are a member of the Church and can be saved.

A classic example of this is the person born and raised on a deserted island. They never heard of Jesus, the Scriptures or even God. But, nonetheless, they perceived a still small but clear voice in their conscience to "do this" and to "avoid that." If they listen, they are responding to grace. If they do not, they are rejecting salvation. And if they do respond, they are, in a very real way, an anonymous Christian whether they realize it or not! So if an atheist is an atheist "through no fault of his own," then he can be saved. If, however, he is an atheist because of a hardness of heart and a refusal to listen even to the voice of God in his conscience, then he will not be saved.

The same is true for all world religions. We do not reject anything of other religions that is true. For example, if someone were to say, "My religion teaches we should love all people." We'd say, "Great!" By the fact they accept this truth, a truth which is true not because it is taught by another religion but simply because it *is* true, they are responding to grace and are partially members of the one Church of Christ!

But the same principle applies to them just as it did to the atheist. If they stay in their religion and fail to discover the Christian truths of salvation in an explicit way because they are stubborn or close-minded, then we have a problem. But if, "through no fault of their own," they fail to discover these truths but only seek the truths of God that just so happen to also be in their religion, then they too are on the road to salvation and are, to a certain degree, members of the Church.

Non-Catholic Christians are the same way. They know Christ Jesus. They have the Scriptures. They pray and worship the Triune God. But they do fail to grasp certain aspects of the fullness of faith. They also are members of the one Church of Christ insofar as they are united to the truths of the faith. Though they do not have the fullness of the faith as revealed by Christ through the Catholic Church, they are, nonetheless, members of the Church of Christ as long as they are authentically following Him in their conscience and not rejecting this fullness of faith through their own fault.

And, truth be told, just because someone is Catholic does not mean they are necessarily a full member of the Church of Christ either. It's not enough to be Catholic in name. It must be in practice. Catholics have an incredible gift, the greatest of the gifts, in that they have the fullness of the faith given explicitly, as well as the means to attain that grace in the Sacraments. But just because we have this gift, it doesn't necessarily follow that we use it!

Lastly, it must be said that those who have been entrusted with the Gospel, especially those Catholics entrusted with the fullness of the faith, are called to spread the explicit message of our faith so as to bring everyone into the Church of Christ and even into the Catholic Church itself. We are called to be missionaries at home, at work, abroad, in the public square and everywhere. We need to understand that it is our duty and privilege to share the Good News with all!

In the end, all are welcome and all are called to come to the fullness of faith in Christ and to live it not only in their conscience but also explicitly, proclaiming the full truths of faith. This is the mission of all and reveals the true meaning of the word "catholic."

Apostolic: Jesus spent three years teaching, performing miracles, and gathering followers. Among those followers were twelve unique individuals called the Apostles. They were called by Jesus to spend extra time with Him, to gain deep insights into His teachings, and then go forth to the ends of the Earth to proclaim the Gospel. In John 20:21, Jesus says to His Apostles after the resurrection:

> As the Father sent me, so now I send you. And when He had said this He breathed on them and said, "Receive the Holy Spirit..."

This begins the apostolic mission of the Church. Jesus was sent to bring the Good News to all. And now He was entrusting this very mission of His to the Apostles. It was now their responsibility to carry this mission out as unique members of the Church acting in the very Person of Christ the Head.

"Apostolic succession" is a term we often use to explain that these twelve Apostles then went and spread the Gospel and passed on this unique mission of being Christ the Head to other Apostles. This continues on until today in the persons of our bishops. Every bishop alive today could technically trace their line of ordination back to the Apostles and to this one moment where Jesus bestowed his grace on the Apostles by breathing the Holy Spirit on them. Priests also share in this mission in a unique way in that they are called to cooperate with the bishop in his ministry.

To be apostolic, the Church must also seek to spread the Gospel to all peoples. This can refer to parents teaching their children how to pray and how to get holy. It can refer to the task of bringing the Gospel into the workplace and society. It can refer to the work of missionaries going abroad sharing the Gospel with those who do not know Christ. The apostolate is a sharing in the one mission of Christ. The mission that the Father sent Him to do. And it is the mission that He, in turn, passed on to the Church. We all share in this mission, so let's get to work!

The Hierarchy and the Pope

Note, first of all, that the word above is "hierarchy" and not "higher-archy." In other words, the hierarchy is not "higher" than others. Rather, it simply has a unique and very sacred calling within the Church. But it's a calling first and foremost of service.

"Hierarchy" means "priestly governance." Hieros = priest, and archy = governance. So it simply means that the Church is set up to be governed, or more properly speaking, shepherded by priests, by those ordained, by those given that special "breath of the Holy Spirit."

The hierarchy is made up especially of the pope and bishops. Priests also share in this role in their unique way by the shepherding of individual churches and people. The hierarchical calling is to specifically share in the mission to shepherd, teach and sanctify the people of God. And it is especially the role of the pope to live this out. Before we look at the threefold mission of the Church to shepherd, teach and sanctify, let's first look at the unique role and origin of the pope.

The pope is the successor of Saint Peter. Jesus gave Saint Peter a unique power when He invited Peter to make his profession of faith. Jesus asked Peter who he thought Jesus was, and Peter responded:

You are the Messiah, the Son of the living God. (Mt 16:16)

Jesus then responded to Peter:

Blessed are you, Simon son of Jonah. For flesh and blood has not revealed this to you, but my heavenly Father. And so I say to you, you are Peter, and upon this rock I will build my church, and the gates of the netherworld shall not prevail against it. I will give you the keys to the kingdom of heaven. Whatever you bind on earth shall be bound in heaven; and whatever you loose on earth shall be loosed in heaven. (Mt 16:17–19)

So was Jesus just being complementary to Peter trying to build up his ego? Was He just thanking Peter for acknowledging who He really is? Or was He doing something more? Was He making Peter a promise that would one day come to fulfillment? Certainly it was the latter of these. Jesus was telling Peter that he would become the rock foundation of the Church and that Peter would enjoy a unique spiritual power of the Keys of Heaven. Whoa! What an incredible gift that was!

Jesus says, "Whatever you bind on earth will be bound in Heaven…" This is no small gift to have. And we should take this as a literal commitment from Jesus to Peter. So, when Jesus did found His Church, when He did "breathe" on the Apostles after His resurrection, He also bestowed this promised gift of supreme authority within His Church to Peter—the power to bind and loose.

I'm sure that, at first, Peter did not fully understand this unique gift. Perhaps as the Church began, within the first few years, the other Apostles would have been reminded, by the Holy Spirit, that Jesus said this. Perhaps Peter, in his humility, would also have been reminded by the Holy Spirit that Jesus said this. And as time went on, there should be no doubt that Peter began to embrace and own this unique gift of supreme authority. We see the first clear exercise of this authority in Acts 15, at the Council of Jerusalem, when there was a disagreement about circumcision. After much debate, Peter stood up and spoke with authority. From there, others followed, and we see that the question they were debating was clarified and settled.

From that time on, the Apostles continued their work of teaching, shepherding and sanctifying. Peter eventually went to Rome to preach and to become the first bishop there. It is in Rome that he died, and it was every successor of the Apostle Peter, in Rome, who took on this unique gift of the supreme authority within the Church. Certainly Jesus did not intend this gift of supreme authority to last only as long as Peter lived. That's why we see this authority passed on to all his successors who are the bishops of Rome. And that's why we call our Church the Roman Catholic Church. Interestingly, if Peter would have gone to Malta or Jerusalem or Asia, we would today most likely have the Maltese or Jerusalem or Asian Catholic Church instead. So the Church is Roman primarily because that's where Peter went; therefore, that's where the supreme authority lies.

Over the centuries, we have come to understand this unique gift of supreme authority and have defined it more clearly. It means that Saint Peter, and all his successors, enjoy full and immediate authority to teach definitively on faith and morals and to govern, or shepherd, according to the mind and will of Christ. So if the pope says something is true regarding faith or morals, then quite frankly it is true. And if he makes a decision on the governance of the Church, then quite simply that's what God wants done. It's as simple as that.

This gift of supreme authority, in regard to teaching on faith and morals, is called "infallibility." It's used in various ways. The most powerful way it's used is when the pope speaks "ex cathedra" or "from the chair." This means symbolically from the Chair of Peter. In this case, he teaches what's called a "dogma" of the faith. Every dogma is true and certain, and we are bound in faith to believe. For example, in 1950 the pope spoke "ex cathedra" about the Assumption of Mary into Heaven. With that declaration, we are bound in conscience to believe. Mary truly was taken body and soul into Heaven upon the completion of her earthly life. Period!

Of course, this power does not apply to those things that have nothing to do with faith and morals. So if the pope says he believes that Argentina will win the next World Cup, then he is only hoping, and I wouldn't go bet all your money on them. He has no special grace to teach things of that nature. But wouldn't it be fun if he did!

The Threefold Office to Preach, Sanctify and Shepherd

As has been mentioned, there is a threefold responsibility that the hierarchy shares in. They are entrusted with the responsibility to preach, shepherd, and sanctify. Each one of these responsibilities is prefigured in the Old Testament and are ultimately fulfilled in Jesus. And each one of these are fulfilled in Jesus in a twofold way. Jesus becomes the great Teacher as well as the Truth that is taught, He becomes the great Shepherd as well as the Sheepfold for the sheep (that's us!) leading us to Himself, and He becomes the great Sanctifier (the one who frees us from sin and redeems us) as well as the means by which we are sanctified (by His sacrifice on the Cross). The clergy share in this threefold mission of Jesus and continue His actual work. Let's look at each.

Preach: In the Old Testament, we saw that God began to teach us through the law given to Moses and also through the ministry of the great prophets. They spoke God's word and began to lay the foundation for the coming Messiah who would teach us all Truth. In fact, Jesus Himself is identified as the fullness of Truth itself.

Jesus, throughout His life, gave a definitive interpretation of the law and the prophets. This is, in part, what upset the religious leaders of His time. Jesus taught as one with authority. And this was an authority that the religious leaders of the time could not accept because of their pride. He definitively interpreted the Old Testament law and the prophets and gave even greater insight into the revealed truths of Heaven. He spoke of salvation, new life, His Father, and so much more! He identified Himself as "the way and the truth and the life." And that "No one comes to the Father except through me" (Jn 14:6).

This authority to teach the Truth, to teach that He is the fulfillment of all Truth, and that He is the Truth itself, was subsequently passed on to the Apostles, who passed it on to the presbyters (priests) who assisted them. It was even passed on, to a certain degree, to deacons. All clergy share in the ability to teach with authority, which is a fascinating gift!

Here is one way to see this gift. Say a lay person teaches a truth of the Gospel. And then say that an ordained minister teaches that exact same truth. Is there a difference? Well, yes. The difference is that, even though the content taught is the same, the ordained minister teaches it with a unique authority. This, in a sense, adds weight to the teaching. But the contrary is true also. Say a lay person teaches some error of the faith. And then say an ordained minister teaches that same error. Is there a difference? Again, the answer is yes. The difference is that when the ordained minister teachers the error it is not only an error but is also, by virtue of his ordination and sacred authority, a certain sacrilege. So it's either a double grace when it's the Truth or a double whammy when it's an error.

Teaching with authority comes in the form of catechesis, individual counseling, and in the celebration of the Liturgy. Preaching within the Liturgy itself is the highest form of preaching and teaching and has potential to produce the most abundant of fruit (or damage if what is taught is erroneous).

Sanctify: Sanctifying means making holy. It means one's sins are forgiven and there is a true reconciliation. This is seen in the Old Testament especially in the various animal sacrifices that took place. The priests of God, from Abraham to all the levitical priests who acted in accord with the law, offered sacrifices to God. These animal sacrifices (lambs, goats, doves, etc.) could not actually take away sins. Rather, they were a way of prefiguring what was to come. They were signs of the one and perfect Lamb of God who would come and offer Himself as the perfect and only sacrifice that took away all sin. Jesus, then, becomes both the perfect and ultimate High Priest as well as the perfect and ultimate Lamb of Sacrifice. And it is through His offering, the offering of Himself, that sins are wiped away.

Jesus instituted the gift of the Most Holy Eucharist as a perpetual sharing in this one Sacrifice of Himself as both Priest and Victim—the one who offers the Sacrifice and the one who is offered as the Sacrifice. His Cross becomes the altar, and His death is the atonement of all sin.

By offering this one Sacrifice of Himself within the context of the Passover Meal (the Last Supper), He forever perpetuated this one Sacrifice for all people for all time to come. At that Passover Meal, He told His Apostles to "do this in remembrance of me." This "remembrance" was not just some command to His Apostles to tell His story and to do what He did so as to help people *remember* what He did. Rather, the meaning of this "remembrance" is that when they actually "do this," they will be inviting everyone present to actually share in that one and eternal Passover Meal! Therefore, every time the Apostles would "do this," they would be making that one Sacrifice of Jesus present, in a real but veiled way, to those who share in it. Over time this was understood as a Sacrament. A Sacrament is a repeating of certain signs and actions that actually accomplishes what it signifies (see *Catechism* #1155). In other words, the celebration of the Eucharist actually makes us present at the Last Supper, and we share in the fruits of this one and only eternal Sacrifice of Christ the High Priest and Victim! It's as if we enter into a time machine each time we participate in the Liturgy and are brought to this extraordinary moment of grace.

When Jesus gave His Apostles the command to "do this in remembrance of me," He was commanding them to sanctify (to make holy) His people by bringing them the great Gift of sanctity and holiness. He was commanding them to bring His priestly Sacrifice to everyone. The Apostles, in turn, passed this grace and command on to all who would follow them in their role as bishops, and each bishop passes this authority on to the priests who minister with him.

This power to sanctify is uniquely given only to priests and bishops and is seen first and foremost in the Eucharist. But it is also seen in every Sacrament that is offered, because every Sacrament takes its power from the one Sacrifice of Christ the High Priest and Victim. Deacons share in this office insofar as they administer Sacraments such as Baptism, which brings forth grace. But the power to stand in the Person of Christ at Mass is unique to the office of priest and bishop.

Shepherd: From the beginning of time, God began to raise up certain leaders who would be images of the one and eternal Shepherd. From Noah, Abraham and Moses, to the great Kings such as David, God called certain leaders who would act as prefigurements of Himself who would come as the true and perfect Shepherd. Jesus, of course, becomes this one Shepherd.

To shepherd is to lead and govern with a spiritual authority. This is ultimately not just an earthly governance but is first and foremost a spiritual governance of the spiritual and eternal Kingdom. It's a governance of our souls, our society, the Church, and ultimately a governance of the world to come! The Kingdom of Heaven, the Kingdom of the New Heavens and New Earth which is promised, is the final place of this governance.

However, Jesus passed on this authority to act in His name and with His authority to the Apostles, who in turn passed it on to their successors, who in turn pass this on to their priests. Deacons do not properly share in the role of governance. Rather, they are called to the ministry of service first and foremost.

Those ordained ministers who share in this ministry of shepherding take on the responsibility first to shepherd souls. This means that God acts through these priests and bishops in such a way that individual people are led by them to God. Furthermore, some priests are chosen to exercise this shepherding authority over a community in that they become pastors of a particular church. There are assisting priests (Associate Pastors) who then assist those pastors.

Bishops are entrusted with the role of shepherding entire dioceses (a gathering of various local parishes). They are the true shepherds of these communities and rely on the assistance of pastors for the fulfillment of their work.

The Laity

It is not only the ordained minister who shares in the threefold office of Jesus to preach, sanctify and shepherd. The laity do so also in their own way. By "laity" we refer to everyone who is not a bishop, priest or deacon. We call this participation of the laity in the threefold office of Christ the "Royal Priesthood." This phrase comes from the First Letter of St. Peter 2:9, "But you are a chosen race, a royal priesthood, a holy nation, a people of his own..."

The primary role of the faithful is to bring the Gospel into the public square. They are on the front line of the Church in the world. Therefore, it's not first and foremost the role of bishops and priests to go out into the world and transform it. The ordained do this especially within the Church. The laity, in turn, do this first and foremost in the world. The *Catechism* quotes Vatican II in proclaiming the following:

> "By reason of their special vocation it belongs to the laity to seek the kingdom of God by engaging in temporal affairs and directing them according to God's will.... It pertains to them in a special way so to illuminate and order all temporal things with which they are closely associated that these may always be effected and grow according to Christ and may be to the glory of the Creator and Redeemer" (LG 31 § 2). (*CCC* #898)

How do they do this? How do they share in this threefold office of Christ? Let's take a look at their unique participation:

Preach: By virtue of their baptism and strengthened by their confirmation, the laity are called to bring the Gospel to the ends of the Earth. They are especially called to transform society by bringing the truths of the Gospel and the natural law wherever they go. It is their right and responsibility to bring the truths of human dignity and even the truths of salvation everywhere. They must also strive to bring the Gospel and natural truths into all laws, social contexts, entertainment, and all else that affects humanity. Furthermore, parents take on a unique responsibility of teaching their children the truths of faith and human dignity.

Sanctify: Parents have the unique responsibility to see to it that their children come to meet Christ Jesus, are baptized, are raised in the practice of the faith and continually enter into a deeper conversion as they grow and mature. Each person is also first and foremost responsible for his or her own soul. This responsibility includes seeking the truths of God, following the moral law and seeking personal sanctity (holiness).

Shepherd: This role is also fulfilled by parents in the way mentioned above in that they must lead their children to faith. They are also called to establish good order in their home, making it a truly Christian environment which fosters the conversion of the whole family. Christians must also engage the social and political order knowing that God is the ultimate Lawgiver and that His laws, especially the natural laws of human dignity which are understood by human reason alone, are established in the civil laws of each community. They are especially entrusted with the task of making sure that laws which trample human dignity are overturned.

Consecrated Life

Among the many ways the laity are called to live out their vocation is the way of consecrated life. There are some who are called to follow Christ in a "more intimate" way of life in which they are dedicated to God alone. Most lay people are called to love God primarily by loving their families. Consecrated life is a calling to love God in a more direct way through the evangelical counsels. The most common of the evangelical counsels are poverty, chastity and obedience. These counsels are lived in the context of religious orders, life as a hermit, as consecrated virgins, through secular institutes and through societies of apostolic life.

Religious Life: This is the life of those called to chastity, poverty and obedience within a specific community that, together, fulfills a specific charism within the Church. For example, the Franciscans are a religious order primarily dedicated to preaching, teaching and serving the poor. The Dominicans are called to study and preach. The Missionaries of Charity (the order founded by St. Mother Teresa) primarily serve the poorest of the poor. All of these communities live by certain rules of life and live in harmony together under that rule, with the direction of superiors, fulfilling the mission and charism of their community.

Eremitical life: These are communities of men or women who are called to the evangelical counsels and who are also called to live as hermits. This is a life especially dedicated to silence, solitude, prayer and study. They join in this life together supporting each other in this sacred calling.

Consecrated Virgins: This is a life with a special calling to live celibacy under the direction of the diocesan bishop. A consecrated virgin is a woman who takes on certain vows under the direction of the bishop and lives those vows out individually for the good of the Church.

Secular Institutes and Societies of Apostolic Life: These are unique forms of consecrated life lived out according to their own constitutions and missions for the purpose of the good of society. The consecrated life is a wonderful gift to the Church. Those called to this life act as missionaries of the Gospel in their own unique way. Some actively preach and teach, some serve the needs of others fulfilling the spiritual and corporal works of mercy, and others are called to a life of prayer. But they all act as missionaries of the Gospel in one way or another. And they all are signs to the whole Church of what is truly important in life—total dedication to God in all things.

Consecrated life went through a difficult period in the Church right after Vatican II. But little by little God is reorganizing and restructuring this way of life; therefore, we have much to look forward to in the future!

8

The Glorious and Final Things!

We now turn our eyes toward Heaven! But to do so we must also turn our eyes toward the reality of Hell and Purgatory. All of these realities give us a full picture of the perfect plan of God regarding His mercy as well as His justice.

We begin with what it means to be a saint, and we specifically focus on the Communion of Saints. In a real way, this chapter goes hand in hand with the previous one on the Church. The Communion of Saints contains the entire Church. So, in fact, this chapter could actually be incorporated into the previous one. But we offer it as a new chapter simply as a way of distinguishing this great communion of all the faithful from the Church only upon Earth. And to understand the Communion of Saints, we must also look at the central role of our Blessed Mother as the Queen of All Saints.

Communion of Saints: Earth, Heaven and Purgatory

What is the Communion of Saints? Properly speaking, it refers to three groupings of people:

1) Those on Earth—The Church Militant;

2) The saints in Heaven—The Church Triumphant;

3) The souls in Purgatory—The Church Suffering.

The unique focus of this section is the "communion" aspect. We are called to be in union with each and every member of Christ. There is a spiritual bond with one another insofar as we are each individually united with Christ. Let's start with those on Earth (the Church Militant) as a continuation of the previous chapter on the Church.

The Church Militant: What brings about our unity more than anything else is the simple but profound fact that we are one with Christ. As explained in the last chapter, this union with Christ happens to varying degrees and in various ways. But, ultimately, every person who is in some way in the grace of God is part of His Body, the Church. This forges a deep union not only with Christ but also with one another.

We see this shared communion manifested in various ways:

–**Faith**: Our shared faith makes us one.

–**Sacraments**: We are each fed by these precious gifts of God's presence in our world.

–**Charism**: Each person is entrusted with unique gifts to be used for the upbuilding of other members of the Church.

–**Common possessions**: The early Church shared their possessions. As members today, we see the need for constant charity and generosity with the goods with which we have been blessed. We are to use them for the good of the Church first and foremost.

–**Charity**: In addition to the sharing of material things, we more importantly share our love. This is charity, and it has the effect of uniting us.

As members of the Church on Earth, then, we are automatically united with each other. This communion with one another goes to the heart of who we are. We were made for unity, and we experience the good fruit of human fulfillment when we experience unity and share in it.

The Church Triumphant: Those who have gone before us and now share in the glories of Heaven, in the Beatific Vision, are not gone. Sure, we do not see them, and we cannot necessarily hear them speak to us in the physical way they did while on Earth. But they are not gone at all. Saint Thérèse of Lisieux said it best when she said, "I want to spend my Heaven doing good on Earth."

The saints in Heaven are in full union with God and make up the Communion of Saints in Heaven, the Church Triumphant! What's important to note, however, is that even though they are enjoying their eternal reward, they are still very much concerned about us.

The saints in Heaven are entrusted with the important task of intercession. Sure, God already knows all our needs, and He could ask us to go directly to Him in our prayers. But the truth is that God wants to use the intercession, and, therefore, the mediation of the saints in our lives. He uses them to bring our prayers to Him and, in return, to bring His grace to us. They become powerful intercessors for us and participators in God's divine action in the world.

Why is this the case? Again, why doesn't God just choose to deal with us directly rather than go through intermediaries? Because God wants all of us to share in His good work and to participate in His divine plan. It would be like a dad who buys a nice necklace for his wife. He shows it to his young children, and they are excited about this gift. The mom comes in and the dad asks the children to bring the gift to her. Now the gift is from her husband, but she will most likely thank her children first for their participation in giving this gift to her. The father wanted the children to be part of this giving, and the mother wanted to make the children a part of her receiving and gratitude. So it is with God! God wants the saints to share in the distribution of His manifold gifts. And this act fills His heart with joy!

The saints also give us a model of holiness. The charity they lived on Earth lives on. The witness of their love and sacrifice was not just a one-time act in history. Rather, their charity is a living reality and continues to have an effect for the good. Therefore, the charity and witness of the saints lives on and affects our lives. This charity in their lives creates a bond with us, a communion. It enables us to love them, admire them and want to follow their example. It is this, coupled with their continuing intercession, which establishes a powerful bond of love and union with us.

The Church Suffering: Purgatory is an often misunderstood doctrine of our Church. What is Purgatory? Is it the place we go to be punished for our sins? Is it God's way of "getting back at us" for the wrong we've done? Is it the result of God's anger? None of these questions really answer the question of Purgatory. Purgatory is nothing other than the burning and purifying love of God in our lives!

When someone dies in God's grace, they are most likely not 100% converted and perfect in every way. Even the greatest of saints would have some imperfection left in their lives. Purgatory is nothing other than that final purification of all remaining attachment to sin in our lives. By analogy, imagine that you had a cup of 100% pure water, pure H_2O. This cup will represent Heaven. Now imagine that you want to add to that cup of water, but all you have is water that is 99% pure. This will represent the holy person who dies with just some slight attachments to sin. If you add that water to your cup, then the cup will now have at least some impurities in the water as it mixes together. The problem is that Heaven (the original cup of 100% H_2O) cannot contain any impurities. Heaven, in this case, cannot have even the slightest attachment to sin in it. Therefore, if this new water (the 99% pure water) is to be added to the cup, it must first be purified even of that last 1% of impurities (attachments to sin). This is ideally done while we are on Earth. This is the process of getting holy. But if we die with any attachment, then we simply say that the process of entering into the final and full vision of God in Heaven will purify us of any remaining attachment to sin. All may already be forgiven, but we may not have detached fully from those sins which were forgiven. Purgatory is the process, after death, of burning out the last of our attachments so that we can enter Heaven 100% freed of everything to do with sin. If, for example, we still have a bad habit of being rude or sarcastic, even those tendencies and habits must be purged.

How does this happen? We do not know. We only know it does. But we also know it's the result of God's infinite love that frees us of these attachments. Is it painful? Most likely. But it's painful in the sense that letting go of any disordered attachment is painful. It's hard to break a bad habit. It's even painful in the process. But the end result of true freedom is worth any pain we may have experienced. So, yes, Purgatory is painful. But it's a sort of sweet pain that we need and it produces the end result of a person 100% in union with God.

Now since we are talking about the Communion of Saints, we also want to make sure to understand that those going through this final purification are still in communion with God, with those members of the Church on Earth, and with those in Heaven. For example, we are called to pray for those in Purgatory. Our prayers are effective. God uses those prayers, which are acts of our love, as instruments of His grace of purification. He allows us and invites us to participate in their final purification by our prayers and sacrifices. This forges a bond of union with them. And no doubt the saints in Heaven especially offer prayers for those in this final purification as they await full communion with them in Heaven. It's a glorious thought and a joy to see how God has orchestrated this entire process for the ultimate purpose of the sacred communion to which we are called!

A Sad Note about Hell

Hell is a sad reality. But it can often be misunderstood. Is Hell a place of eternal punishment for those who have turned from God? Well, yes and no. No in the sense that God does not act in a punitive way out of His wrath. He doesn't want to "get even" with those who reject Him. Rather, Hell is a result of one's own free choice to turn from God. And God is a gentleman! What I mean is that God will not impose Heaven on someone who rejects it. If someone rejects the love of God, then God will allow that person, by his/her own free will, to experience the effects of that rejection. And the effects are Hell.

Hell is a sad place where one is alone with the "unholy trinity": me, myself and I. It's an eternal existence of isolation and a complete loss of communion with God and others. Some popular rock bands misrepresent Hell as a place of partying all night long! It's as if everyone who goes to Hell is in for a great party with the devil and his minions. But this is so far from the truth. Hell is not a party, and people in Hell will not like each other or even share in any form of communion with each other. Hell is a state where there is no love, only hate. There will be complete isolation and self-pity. There will be no friendship and no get togethers. Hell is a sad place and a sad state to be in. It's a complete loss of God and an eternal existence without that love of God.

Hell is chosen by our actions just as Heaven is chosen by our actions. It's not enough to simply say, "Jesus, save me!" No, if we say we want to go to Heaven but then choose to turn from God 100% by our actions, we will then remain in this state of 100% loss of God for eternity. Ouch! Don't let that happen. More will be said about this process of entering eternal damnation in the third book of this series: *My Catholic Morals!* In that book, we will focus on the reality of mortal sin. But for now it's sufficient to see that Hell is real and to understand what this reality is all about.

The Final Age to Come

In Chapter 5 we reflected upon the effects of Jesus' death and resurrection. We pondered the reality of the resurrection of the body and the new Heavens and Earth we are called to share in. This section will be a summary of those important points highlighting especially the reality of the new Heavens and Earth that await us!

Heaven and Purgatory, as they now exist, are not the end game for God. Jesus will one day return in all His glory and transform all things into His new and glorious Kingdom. Those in Heaven will be reunited with their new transformed earthly bodies. Those on Earth, who are living in God's grace, will also instantly be purified of all attachment to sin and receive their glorified bodies. In this moment, Heaven and Earth will become one. There will be a glorious transformation of both, and they will be the one and complete dwelling place of God and all His saints. And we will share in this new life, body and soul forever.

What will this new life look like? No one knows. As mentioned in Chapter 5, there are many symbolic images of this in the Book of Revelation. Read Chapters 21–22 from the Book of Revelation to get a picture of how the Apostle John saw it in his vision. This is mysterious language, but it is also true language. True in the sense that it reveals the mystery of this new existence in a veiled, symbolic and glorious way. It is real; we just have a hard time fully grasping what it says. But that's OK! We will find out one day if we keep on the path of holiness!

This new world will be a place where "there shall be no more death or mourning, wailing or pain..." (Rv 21:4). All disorder in nature, such as disease and suffering, will be destroyed. Our disordered minds, passions, desires, etc., will be newly ordered, and all will be glorious. We will live the human lives God intended for all eternity. We will be fully united with Him and with each other. And we can be assured that we will never get bored!

We must make this our goal and our constant hope. This is why we are here. We are on a journey, and the new Heavens and Earth are our final destination. Now is the time we choose the path we are on, and now is the time to move continually to this glorious fulfillment of our human lives. Don't miss out!

Our Blessed Mother: The Queen of All Saints!

The best way to conclude this volume is to reflect upon the final and glorious role of our Blessed Mother as the Queen and Mother of all the saints in this new age to come. She already played an essential role in the salvation of the world, but her work is not over. By her Immaculate Conception, she became the perfect instrument of the Savior and, as a result, the new Mother of all the living. As this new mother, she undoes the disobedience of Eve by her continual free choice of perfect cooperation with and obedience to God's divine plan. At the Cross, Jesus gave His mother to John, which is a symbol of the fact that He gave her to all of us as our new mother. Therefore, insofar as we are members of the Body of Christ, members of the Body of her Son, we are also, by the necessity of God's plan, children of this one mother.

One of the Dogmas of our faith is that upon the completion of her life on Earth, our Blessed Mother was taken body and soul into Heaven to be with her Son for all eternity. And now, from her place in Heaven, she is given the unique and singular title of Queen of All the Living! She is the Queen of the Kingdom of God now, and she will be Queen of this Kingdom for all eternity!

As Queen, she also enjoys the unique and singular gift of being the mediatrix and distributor of grace. It's best understood like this:

–She was preserved from all sin at the moment of her Immaculate Conception;

–As a result, she was the only fitting human instrument by which God could take on flesh;

–God the Son did take on flesh through her by the power and working of the Holy Spirit;

–Through this one divine Son, now in the flesh, the salvation of the world came about;

–This gift of salvation is transmitted to us through grace. Grace comes primarily through prayer and the sacraments;

–THEREFORE, since Mary was the instrument through which God entered our world, she is also the instrument through which ALL grace comes. She is the instrument of all that resulted from the Incarnation. Therefore, she is the Mediatrix of Grace!

In other words, Mary's act of mediation for the Incarnation was not just some historical act that took place long ago. Rather, her motherhood is something that is continuous and eternal. It is a perpetual motherhood of the Savior of the world and is a perpetual instrumentality of all that comes to us from this Savior.

God is the source, but Mary is the instrument. And she is the instrument because God wanted it this way. She can do nothing by herself, but she doesn't have to do it by herself. She is not the Savior. She is the instrument.

As a result of this, we must see her role as glorious and essential in the eternal plan of salvation. Devotion to her is a way of simply acknowledging what is true. It's not just some honor we bestow upon her by thanking her for cooperating with God's plan. Rather, it's an acknowledgment of her continual role of mediation of grace in our world and in our lives.

From Heaven, God does not take this from her. Rather, she is made our Mother and our Queen. And a worthy Mother and Queen she is!

Small Group Study

One of the best ways to learn our glorious Catholic faith is through faith-based, small-group discussion and study. Talking about our faith brings clarity. Hearing what others have to say brings insight.

Each of the three books of the *My Catholic Life! Series* can be used as an eight-week program of Catholic study for you to engage in. This small group study program is great for these and other settings:

–**Family**—Why not gather family members together for an eight-week study of our faith?!

–**Friends**—Initiate a study among your friends and invite some new friends!

–**Neighborhood**—This is a great way to evangelize right in your neighborhood. Send a letter out inviting neighbors. You just may be surprised at how many are interested!

–**Parish**—Talk to your parish priest to gain permission to begin one or more study groups at your local church.

–**R.C.I.A.**—This is a great tool to use for those becoming Catholic. All three series, together, will cover the entire *Catechism*!

Who can start a program?—This program is designed to be easy for any Catholic to organize and lead. You do not have to be an expert in the Catholic faith to take the initiative. If you feel called to take this initiative, then "Be not afraid" and jump in!

What do you need?—The materials include one of the three catechetical books from the *My Catholic Life! Series* as well as the study companion which is available for free online. So visit that link, pray, and ask our Lord how He wants you to help spread the faith!

Also, download the "My Catholic Life!" app for smartphones and tablets. Available from our website or all app stores.

Visit our website for more information:

www.mycatholic.life